MARIACHIARA POZZANA

THE GARDENS OF FLORENCE AND TUSCANY

COMPLETE GUIDE

Project and editorial coordination: Camilla Giunti
Editorial manager: Roberto De Meo
Graphic design: Leonardo Di Bugno
Layout: Stefania Cinotti
Editing: Alessandra Pelagotti
Translation: Catherine Frost
Drawings of the gardens: Cristina Basaldella
for the studio Architettura e Paesaggio by
Mariachiara Pozzana
Maps: Legenda, Novara

Photographs: Nicola Grifoni, Florence (p. 11);
Fondazione Collodi (p. 105); Alessandro Tombel-
li, Firenze (pp. 77, 160, 161s, 168); Archivio
Giunti, Firenze (pp. 14, 55, 87); Archivio Pozzolini,
Florence (pp. 98 e 99b).
Unless otherwise indicated, the photographs
belong to Archivio Giovanni Breschi, Florence.

Acknowledgements:
The author wishes to thank all those who have
collaborated in the realization of this book
as well as the owners of villas and gardens who
have made their property available
for photographs and information, in particular:
Livia Aldobrandini Pediconi, Anna Balsamo,
Maria Teresa Benedetti, Ferdinando e Laura
Budini Gattai, Massimo Canizza, Filippo
e Giorgiana Corsini, Vittoria Colonna, Gil Cohen
e Paul Gervais, Giovanna Donato, Giuliano Gori,
Lorenza Stucchi Prinetti, Luisa Oliva, Francesca
Grabau, Anna Marchi, Carla Mazzei, Paolo
Peyron, Paola ed Anna Porcinai, Vanni Pozzolini,
Alberto Sandrelli e Maria Sofia Sandrelli Duranti,
Lorenzo Scaretti, Andrea Scavetta, Daniel
Spoerri †, Vieri Torrigiani, Luigi Zalum.

As well as the Bureaus: Soprintendenza ai Beni
Ambientali Architettonici Artistici e Storici di Pisa,
Soprintendenza ai Beni Ambientali Architettonici
Artistici e Storici di Arezzo, Soprintendenza
ai Beni Ambientali e Architettonici di Firenze,
Soprintendenza ai Beni Ambientali
e Architettonici di Siena, Orto Botanico di Firenze,
Associazione Dimore Storiche della Toscana,
Cassa di Risparmio di Pisa, Fondazione Parchi
Monumentali Bardini e Peyron, promossa
da Ente Cassa di Risparmio di Firenze,
Fondazione Nazionale Carlo Collodi, Direzione
Sezione Ambiente del Comune di Firenze, New
York University, Villa La Pietra.
A sincere thanks to friends: Pier Francesco
Bernacchi, Sandro Di Mare, Maria Rita ed Enrico
Guadagni, François Roche †.

Thanks also, for their continuous collaboration, to:
Giuseppe Bagnoli; for invaluable information on
citrus trees Paolo Galeotti; for the photographic
material kindly made available: Alessandro
Tombelli; for having furnished the material for the
following texts: Tessa Matteini (Orti Oricellari,
Giardino Corsi, Villa Caruso, Giardino Catastini,
Villa Mansi, Villa Torrigiani, Villa Oliva, Villa Grabau,
Palazzo Pfanner, Giardino dei Tarocchi) Tiziana
Grifoni (Orto Botanico, Villa Bibbiani, Cetinale,
Geggiano, Castello di Brolio, Abbazia di
Coltibuono, Fonterutoli) e Arianna Bechini
(Giardino Garzoni e Parco di Collodi).

The publisher assumes no responsibility
for any damage or inconvenience occurring
in connection with the information contained
in this guide.
Since much of the information is subject to change,
readers are advised to inquire in advance before
a visit.
The editorial staff will be grateful to anyone,
either readers or experts in the field, who notifies
us of errors or outdated information found in the
guide.

www.giunti.it

© 2011 Giunti Editore S.p.A.
Via Bolognese 165 - 50139 Firenze - Italy
Via Dante 4 - 20121 Milano - Italy
First edition: september 2001

Reprint	Year
6 5 4 3 2 1 0	2014 2013 2012 2011

Printed by Giunti Industrie Grafiche S.p.A. - Prato

CONTENTS

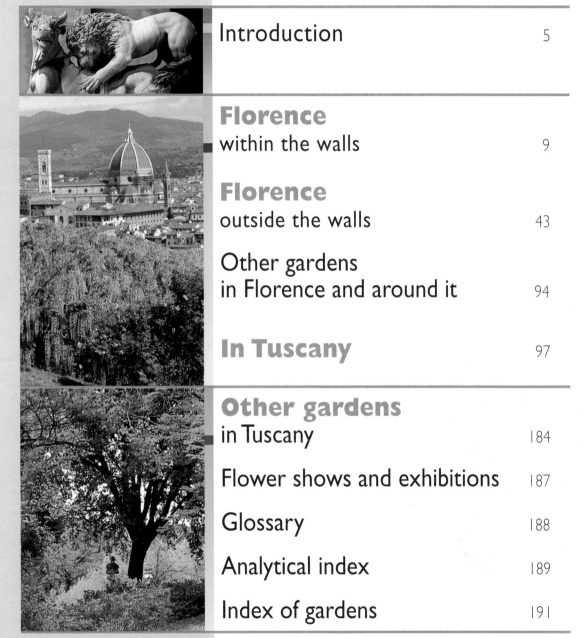

Introduction   5

Florence
within the walls   9

Florence
outside the walls   43

Other gardens
in Florence and around it   94

In Tuscany   97

Other gardens
in Tuscany   184

Flower shows and exhibitions   187

Glossary   188

Analytical index   189

Index of gardens   191

Introduction

Tuscany boasts an extraordinary number of villas and gardens. From the 15th century on, gardens were created for palaces or more often villas, in both city and countryside, practically without interruption. This is a region where nature merges with art, the past with the present. A garden calls for great care and attention; maintaining it is frequently expensive. Ancient gardens in particular, those that everyone would like to see, are hard to keep up and often difficult to visit. But to find the 'key' to the garden, to enter a world so wonderful, always fully compensates for the minor difficulties encountered.

The heritage of Tuscan gardens is invaluable both for quantity and for the vast range of chronology and types, spanning a period stretching from the Middle Ages to our own day and embracing situations that are totally different in form, significance and inspiration.

Visiting the gardens of Tuscany is thus a journey in time as well as in space. First comes the Medieval monastic garden, as exemplified by the herb garden of Coltibuono, designed for the monastery's kitchen and pharmacy, where plants were grown not only for their properties but also for their religious and symbolic nature. Next came the first villa garden in the modern sense, exemplified by that of the Trebbio Castle in Mugello.

The Medieval herb garden model began to change, becoming more refined, with much longer pergolas, adorned by stone capitals, and perspectives opening out to find a new relationship with the surrounding landscape. But it was only with the creation of the Medicean villas, at Fiesole, Careggi and Poggio a Caiano, that the modern model for a garden was established – a place that is both botanical collection and outdoor museum, adorned with ancient and contemporary works of art. The new villa garden fit harmoniously into the landscape, according to

At left:
the garden of Boboli,
pool of the Isolotto,
with the fountain
of Oceanus *and,*
in the background,
the cypress avenue.

the suggestions of Leon Battista Alberti's *De re aedificatoria*, a famous treatise written in the mid-15th century. The Piccolomini palace garden at Pienza, apparently a walled Medieval garden, a *hortus conclusus*, in reality opens onto the valley in highly innovative manner, testifying to the new humanistic sensitivity.

The 16th century Medicean gardens at Castello, Boboli and Pratolino formed models imitated all over Europe. At the time of the Grand Dukes the garden became an image of political power, assuming complex allegorical meanings, often expressed in grottoes and nymphaeums. Orchards, *ragnaie* for bird-catching, and *boschetti*, or little groves of trees, imposed form on gardens embellished by flowers. Water, essential for irrigation, was collected in ponds or basins and used in various ways for *giochi d'acqua*, or waterworks. Water is the element on which a garden lives, and from which every splendid effect derives. In 1599 the Flemish painter Justus Utens depicted the Medicean gardens in famous lunettes, fixing their image in that golden age which seems to represent the highest peak of Tuscan horticulture.

In the history of the art of gardening, Florence is not the only city in Tuscany to display masterpieces. Gardens based on precise canons but distinguished by different and entirely original materials, types and botanical species were created in the State of Lucca, independent of Florence. In the Sienese territory, subjected to Florence, magnificent examples of garden art have survived from the 16th and 17th centuries, many of them created by Baldassare Peruzzi, the architect who designed such masterpieces as the villa and garden of Vicobello.

In the late 17th and early 18th century the fashion arose for architectural, perspective gardens, designed together with the villa to form a consistent, scenic whole. This was the time of the Baroque garden masterpieces such as Villa Garzoni and Villa Gamberaia. These are of different scenic impact: the first is monumental, the second arouses a sense of intimacy. The model of the terraced garden reappeared in the mid-18th century in the Capponi garden at Florence, and elements of the

16th century garden, the fruit orchard and the *ragnaia*, returned again during this same period in the villa garden La Quiete in Florence.

Still in the 18th century the beautiful Val d'Esse, in the Cortona region, assumed the rationalizing aspect still to be seen today, with the flourishing of gardens of agricultural type, incorporating farm structures within them (a fine example is the Passerini garden at Pergo). The vogue for the romantic garden, derived from the English landscape garden, came late to Tuscany, but was no less significant for this reason. The first masterpieces, the Corsi garden and the Torrigiani garden, appeared in Florence. But the entire region was swept by the naturalist orientation of the English garden and nature, but nature always recreated by the gardener's art. Many Medicean parks, such as those of Castello and Petraia, were transformed in keeping with the new style, and Pratolino became the most important landscape park in Tuscany. In the Lucca region as well Baroque gardens underwent major changes, often due to the Napoleonic domination and intense contacts with contemporary French culture. The new landscape park of Villa Marlia, one of the finest in Italy, harmoniously co-exists with the older gardens. It was in the romantic period that the vogue for botanical collecting swept through Tuscany. The Lucchese collections of trees became famous, with camellias the pride of the area. In Florence too horticulture was promoted by numerous collectors and expert gardeners.

The early 20th century marked the revival of the Italian formal garden. Cecil Pinsent, the English landscape architect, was responsible for the most extraordinary reinterpretations of the Renaissance and the Baroque garden, at I Tatti and at Villa Le Balze in Florence, and at Foce in Chianciano.

In the 1930s the young Pietro Porcinai was already active in this field. Born in Florence, he is undoubtedly the greatest Italian landscape artist of the 20th century, the first to rediscover the garden of Italian tradition and reinterpret it in a modern sense. From him came the concept of a sober, functional garden, inserted in the landscape and composed of hedges like the Italian formal garden, but modeled in new forms. Some of his most striking and complete creations are the garden of the Apparita in Siena, that of Villa il Roseto in Florence, and the villa garden Il Castelluccio at Santa Croce sull'Arno.

In the decade of the Nineties contemporary art gardens were created. At Celle the romantic park was transformed by systematically inserting contemporary works of art to be displayed outdoors, in harmony with the environment. At Seggiano, near Grosseto, a sculpture garden was created by the Swiss artist Daniel Spoerri; in Maremma, on the border between Tuscany and Lazio, Niki de Saint Phalle created the garden of the Tarocchi; and within the Sterpaia park a number of works by Marcello Guasti were installed.

Lastly, the English tradition of great gardening still lives today in Villa Massei, at the gates of Lucca, allowing us to hope for a revival of the figure of the landscape gardener. And tomorrow...

Mariachiara Pozzana, May 2001

Introduction to the new edition

Tomorrow is already today, and ten years after the first edition of this guide, the world of gardening has opened out to new discoveries and initiatives.
Today in Tuscany we can add to the already vast list of gardens open to visitors important new ones such as the Reinhardt Garden in Cortona and the Ragnaia di San Giovanni d'Asso, as well as some ancient gardens newly opened to the public, such as the Medicean Villa della Magia.
Garden tourism has acquired new importance, and the urge to partake of nature, to discover landscapes, to understand the beauty and meaning of a garden is spreading fast even among those who had never thought of the natural world as a form of art.
In Tuscany too, Grandi Giardini Italiani has created an important circuit of gardens open to visitors, which includes Boboli, the Bardini Garden and many others.

If it is true that a garden expresses, like a biological marker, the level of a civilization, we may feel at least a little optimistic, to see flourishing gardens waving like shining banners above the problematical panorama of today.

Mariachiara Pozzana, February 2011

NOTE
The gardens described in this guide have been selected on the basis of factors such as accessibility to the public, historical and botanical importance, beauty, contemporary realization, and state of conservation. Some gardens have been excluded since they cannot be visited. The difference between gardens described at length and those described briefly indicates no difference in value, but is based only on the above considerations. In the case of botanical gardens, now scientific institutions, that of Florence has been described in greater detail, those of Pisa and Lucca more briefly.
The gardens are presented in three sections, concerning three different geographical areas: *Florence within the walls*, *Florence outside the walls* and and *In Tuscany*. Maps show the locations of the gardens and itineraries for visitors.
Most of the articles consist of two parts, one introductive, the other descriptive. Itineraries for visits are also indicated. The boxes beside each article give information on how to reach the garden, how to visit it and the services provided (for private gardens, this information is based on the owners' statements. In villas inhabited by the owners, visits are allowed at the discretion of the residents). Other boxes are dedicated to the history and particular aspects of the garden: descriptions by famous authors, nature of the botanical collections and so on. For the gardens rich in history, chronological data are given. At the end is a list of texts for those who want to know more about the garden.

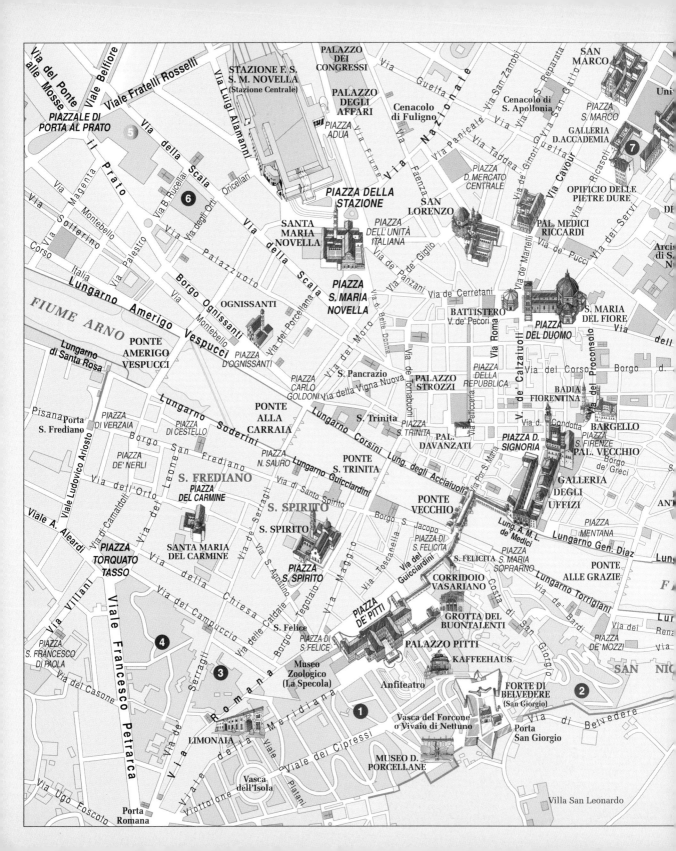

Florence
within the walls

1 Boboli		10
2 Giardino Bardini		19
3 Giardino Corsi (or Annalena)		24
4 Giardino Torrigiani		26
5 Giardino Corsini al Prato		30
6 Orti Oricellari		32
7 Giardino Budini Gattai		34
8 Orto Botanico		36
9 Giardino del Museo archeologico		38

Boboli
A living work of art

Detail of the amphitheater

Pitti Palace was created, then, between 1630 and 1631, the cypress avenue designed by Giulio Parigi was planted.

The construction of the Medicean garden began when Eleonora, wife of Cosimo I, purchased land known at the time as the 'Pitti garden' from the name of the first owners.

Niccolò Pericoli, known as Tribolo, was commissioned to design the garden. The sculptor based its layout on the perspective axis that traverses the entrance to the palace and rises along the hill behind it. In place of what remained of a stone quarry he built an amphitheater divided by *ragnaie* and lined with fruit trees. To the left of the palace a great flower garden was planted.

Numerous artists worked on this magnificent garden. When Tribolo died he was succeeded by Davide Fortini, then, between 1554 and 1561, by Giorgio Vasari followed by Bartolomeo Ammannati (from 1560 to 1583). After 1574 Bernardo Buontalenti was also summoned by Francesco I to work at Boboli.

In the early 17th century Cosimo II decided to extend the garden beyond the bastions erected during the war with Siena. Giulio Parigi, commissioned to enlarge the gardens in 1612, created the cypress avenue. Parigi transformed the garden amphitheatre behind palazzo Pitti into a theatrical space built of masonry in 1630; the work was finished by Alfonso Parigi the Younger.

After some years of abandonment work on the garden resumed in 1765, at a time when the Grand Duchy had passed to the Hapsburg Lorraines.

Boboli is known the world over as one of Italy's most important gardens. So famous that its name alone evokes the idea of a Renaissance garden, Boboli is one of the peak achievements in the Italian art of gardening.

The park as we see it today is chiefly the result of two initiatives; first the 16th century garden behind the

At the initiative of Pietro Leopoldo the *Kaffee-house* was built (1775) as well as the *limonaia* by Zanobi Del Rosso (1777-1778) and the Palazzina della Meridiana by Niccolò Gaspero Paoletti (1776).

In the 19th century the Annalena entrance was built, with a *palazzina* and grotto, and a major change was made in the garden, consisting of destroying the old mazes to make room for the carriage drive designed by Pasquale Poccianti (1834).

Boboli is the model for the garden-museum, a garden created to display ancient and modern statues. It can also be considered the exemplification of a perfect manual on garden art, due to the multitude of elements that, over the course of the centuries, have gone to make up this extraordinary work of art. Along the garden's two main axes – the 16th century one that crosses the amphitheater and goes on to the statue of *Abundance*, and the 17th century one of the cypress avenue – the visitor is struck by examples of garden art as numerous as they are splendid. Outstanding among them are the late 18th century *Kaffeehaus* garden, the turf theater around the Forcone pool and the little Baroque garden of the Cavaliere.

In front of the Palazzina della Meridiana is a second **turf theater**, dramatically dominated by the **marble Pegasus** (coming from the Pratolino park) and a small rose garden in the vicinity of the little Madama grotto, with its imposing statue of *Jove*. Important elements of garden architecture are the great hedges lining the paths through the ancient *selvatici*, or wild areas, and the *ragnaie* in the 17th century part of the garden, a particularly fascinating section of the park. The **Isolotto** in the center of its pool is a splendid Baroque garden on water, created to display potted citrus trees.

For its complex layout and the great number of works of art all over the garden, two different itineraries for visitors are suggested, each of them to be covered in two to three hours.

The Isolotto

First Itinerary

From the Ammannati courtyard
to the Great Grotto by Buontalenti

Behind the severe facade of the Pitti Palace the garden opens out in all its splendor. Closed off by the Moses grotto (which takes its name from the porphyry statue of Moses), the Ammannati courtyard forms an elegant entrance to the park. The grotto was designed to solve the problem of linking spaces on different levels, since the courtyard is lower than the amphitheater behind it. The ramp of stairs to the right of the grotto leads up to the

amphitheater leaving to the left, above the Moses grotto, the fountain of the Artichoke, a work by Francesco Susini (1639-1641).

In front of the fountain is a little geometric garden, from which can be admired the perspective that unites the different levels of the garden, running across the amphitheater and the **Forcone pool** to arrive at the tiered turf theater and the statue of *Abundance*.

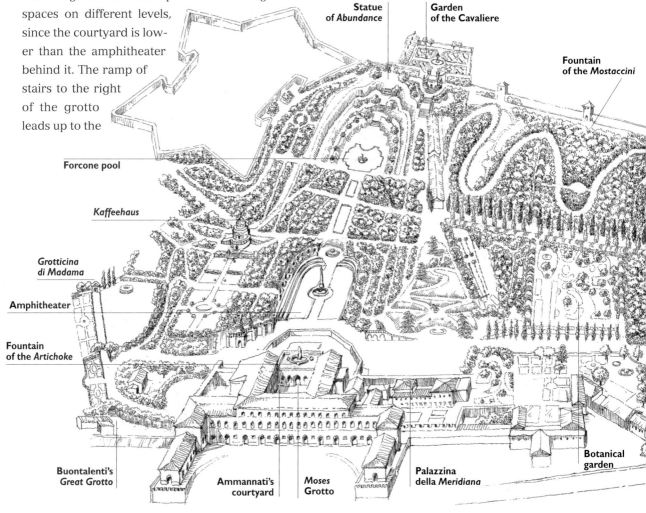

Statue
of *Abundance*

Garden
of the Cavaliere

Fountain
of the *Mostaccini*

Forcone pool

Kaffeehaus

*Grotticina
di Madama*

Amphitheater

Fountain
of the *Artichoke*

Buontalenti's
Great Grotto

Ammannati's
courtyard

Moses
Grotto

Palazzina
della *Meridiana*

Botanical
garden

At the center of the amphitheater is a large granite pool placed there in 1840 by Poccianti and the Egyptian obelisk coming from Villa Medici, erected in Boboli by Paoletti in 1790. The **amphitheater** has six tiers of seats in masonry surmounted by a decorated balustrade. Originally, 24 niches held classical statues with figures of dogs and other animals at the sides. In 1818 Giuseppe Cacialli renovated the amphitheater, placing terracotta urns with imitation marble decoration between the statues.

On the steep slope that leads to the Forcone basin (a semicircular lawn links the first two levels, at the exit from the amphitheater) are the classical statues of a *Togaed Personage*, the *Emperor* and *Ceres*.

The path leads up to what could be called the sec-

Above:
the Palazzina
della Meridiana

Bottom:

Kaffeehaus

a work
by Igor Mitoraj
in the garden

the Forcone *pool*

Pool of the *Isolotto*

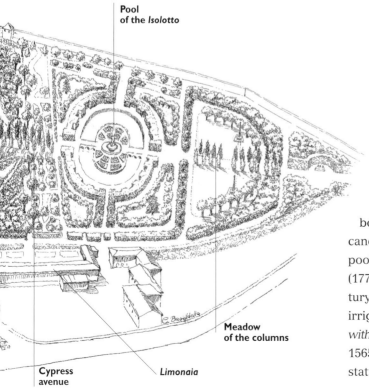

Meadow of the columns

Cypress avenue

Limonaia

ond amphitheater, built of tiers of turf seats and bounded by plane trees pruned to the shape of candelabras. At the center is the great mixtilinear pool designed by the architect Zanobi Del Rosso (1777-1778), who transformed an existing 16th century pool to build this one, used to collect water to irrigate the garden. The bronze statue of *Neptune with Naiads and Tritons* by Stoldo Lorenzi dates from 1565-1568. The central stairway ends at the marble statue of *Abundance*, sculpted by Giambologna in

The grottoes

The most significant element
of the Renaissance grotto
may be the fact that it is a
concrete place of encounter
between art and science.
It was in the grotto
that the most innovative
combinations of materials
were experimented.
The *Grotticina di Madama*
and the *Great Grotto*
of Boboli are among the first
garden grottoes to be built
in Italy (the *Great Grotto* is
now undergoing restoration).
Constructed through a highly
complicated technique,
exposed to the erosive effect
of water and thus requiring
frequent maintenance
operations, the two grottoes
provide documentation
on the environment in which
16th c. gardens were
created, an environment
where science and natural
philosophy, aesthetic caprice
and enchantment were
interwoven to form a
fascinating whole.

The Great Grotto

collaboration with Pietro Tacca and Sebastiano Salvini. The allegorical figure clearly symbolizes the prosperity of the Grand Duchy.

From the statue of *Abundance*, after having admired the splendid panoramic view over the city, the garden and the palace, turn right to find the garden of the Cavaliere (from the name of the bastions erected by Michelangelo in 1529). The little formal garden, in the past planted to medicinal herbs, was rearranged in 1612 by Giulio Parigi, who filled it with rare species. On the same occasion, the big room for vases that now houses the Porcelain Museum was constructed. Today the garden, planted to roses and peonies, is splendid at the flowering season, in late April and early May. Its current design is the work of Giuseppe Del Rosso, who also built the stairway with the ancient statues of the Muses in 1792.

From the garden of the Cavaliere we return to the statue of *Abundance* and descend toward the *Kaf-feehaus*, with the imposing walls of Forte di Belvedere on the left. This elegant little building, commissioned by Pietro Leopoldo di Lorena and designed by Zanobi Del Rosso, reflects the Central European fashion of the times for drinking coffee outdoors. The fine garden in front of the *Kaffeehaus* was originally an orchard. From the central path a number of ancient ilexes can be seen on the right. These great trees are all that remains today of the imposing 16th century *ragnaia*. At the end of the path stands the fountain of *Ganymede* by Stoldo Lorenzi (c. 1550). Continuing to the right along a straight path, we see on the right the marble statue of *Jove* coming from Pratolino. The path leads on to the *Grotticina di Madama*, which can be visited only with permission. Commissioned by Eleonora di Toledo of Davide Fortini and built between 1553 and 1555,

The Forcone Pool, also known as the 'Neptune fishpond'; in the background, the Pitti Palace

the little grotto is distinguished by animal sculptures emerging from the back wall, the work of Baccio Bandinelli and Giovanni Fancelli.

Returning to the broad avenue we descend still further to find Buontalenti's grotto, called the **Great Grotto**, a real chamber of wonders designed to strike the beholder with amazement.

This building, begun by Vasari between 1556 and 1560, was transformed into a rustic grotto by Buontalenti (1583-1593). Along with the Grotticina di Madama it became the model for every grotto built later. The facade is decorated with *spugne*, stuccowork (*Peace and Justice* by Giovanni Battista del Tadda) and statues (*Bacchus and Ceres* by Baccio Bandinelli, 1552-1556). Inside, in half-shadow, figures modeled in stucco, perhaps inspired by the myth of Pyrrhus and Deucalion, seem to emerge from the walls. In the corners two of Michelangelo's *Slaves* struggle to free themselves from the block of marble (these are copies; the originals are now in the Accademia Gallery). Before the grotto is the exit from the garden, known as the *rondò di Bacco* from the marble statue of the *Young Bacchus* by Valerio Cioli (a plaster cast of the original, known also as *Nano Morgante*, is displayed). Not far away are the Roman statues of the *Dacian Prisoners*.

The fountain of Oceanus; in the background the cypress avenue

The 'meadow of the columns'

Second itinerary

*From the level of the amphitheater
to the 'meadow of the columns'*

From the amphitheater lawn we turn right, descending toward the Palazzina della Meridiana by Paoletti and Poccianti. To the right of the palazzina a small camellia garden can be seen from above. From here the path leads up to the right, arriving in the vicinity of the Botanical Garden, open only in summer. The garden, created by Filippo Parlatore between 1841 and 1850 to replace the 18th century *jardin potager* (of which only the pineapple greenhouses remain) has lovely ponds where aquatic plants grow. Through the *cerchiata* of ilexes, a majestic corridor of trees planted between 1612 and 1614, we arrive at the cypress avenue. Descending along the avenue we see on the left the remains of the 17th century mazes, demolished in 1834 to make room for the carriage drive.

The fountain of the Mostaccini, situated along the Medieval city walls, marks the boundary of the *ragnaia of Peace*; decorated with sixteen stone mascarons, the fountain was created by Romolo Ferrucci between 1619 and 1621. The avenue is lined with classical and late 16th century statues. Near the end of the avenue are 17th century sculptures representing various games. We then arrive at the famous **pond of the Isolotto**. An artificial island, elliptical in shape, is laid out as a formal garden with potted lemon trees, antique roses and bulbs and the **fountain of *Oceanus*** by Giambologna (1576).

We then go on to the so-called '**meadow of the columns**'. In the vast semicircular space that closes off the garden to the south, Paoletti placed two column; twelve classical busts adorn the hemicycle.

Further on are a group of 17th century sculptures of grotesque subject, the *Caramogi* by Ferrucci.

From the broad meadow we turn to the right, rising along the avenue that goes back to the Palazzina della Meridiana. On the left is the great *limonaia* built by Zanobi Del Rosso between 1777 and 1778. It is still used today to shelter the five hundred urns of citrus trees in winter. In front of the *limonaia* is a lovely formal garden with antique roses and bulbs. Beyond the *limonaia* a path leads, on the left, to the *Annalena* grotto, the most recent of the Boboli grottoes. Constructed in 1817 by Giuseppe Cacialli, the grotto contains the *Adam and Eve* sculptural group by Michelangelo Naccherino (c. 1616). From here visitors can either exit onto Via Romana or return to the *rondò di Bacco*.

To know more
F. M. Soldini, *Descrizione del giardino di Boboli*, Florence 1789.

Boboli '90. Proceedings of the international symposium of studies for safeguarding and valorizing gardens, Florence, 9-11 March 1989, Florence 1991, Vols. I and II.

Web: www.uffizi.firenze.it/musei/boboli

the vegetation in the garden

The Pegasus and the turf theater

In Boboli, trees, hedges, meadows and flowers are elements of extraordinary interest and enchanting beauty. Cypress avenues and cerchiate of majestic ilexes, green walls that harmoniously delimit space, hedges of box in elaborate geometric patterns, all concur to make the garden not only a living work of art but also an invaluable document of the history of gardening in Italy.

The maintenance of Boboli calls for great effort and professional expertise. Many sections of the park have been restored recently and new plants have been added or used to replace old ones; for example, antique bulbs in the garden on the Isolotto and camellias in the little garden visible from the Palazzina della Meridiana.

Chronology

1549 Eleonora di Toledo, wife of Cosimo I, purchases the 15th century Pitti Palace, already possessing a garden of modest size. The project for the new garden is commissioned of Tribolo who completes, in the words of Giorgio Vasari, "the layout of the mount... accommodating all of the things with fine judgement in their proper places".
1550 Davide Fortini succeeds Tribolo at the death of the latter. The work goes on.
1553-1555 The Grotticina di Madama is constructed.
1574 Buontalenti is appointed director of works in Boboli
1583-1593 The *Great Grotto* is built.
1599 Justus Utens paints a lunette that documents the appearance of the garden at the time.

1630-1634 Giulio Parigi and his son Alfonso transform the 'garden amphitheater' into a building. The garden is extended to the south toward Porta Romana. It now includes the 16th century bastions erected under Cosimo I. The cypress avenue, the labyrinths, the *ragnaie* and the pool with the Isolotto are built.
1636 The statue of *Abundance*, begun by Giambologna and finished by Tacca, is placed in the position it still occupies today.
1637 The statue of *Oceanus*, a work by Giambologna, adorns the Isolotto.
c. 1637-1641 Francesco Susini creates the fountain of the *Artichoke*, placed above the Moses Grotto.
1737 The Botanical Garden is created, linked to the museum of natural history 'La Specola'.
1766 The *jardin potager*, or cutting garden, is created, famous for its pineapple greenhouse.

1774-1775 The *Kaffeehaus* is built to the design of Zanobi Del Rosso.
1777-1778 An orange house is built to replace the old seraglio. Changes are made in the pool surrounding the fountain of the Forcone.
1790 The Egyptian obelisk is placed at the center of the amphitheater on a base designed by Niccolò Gaspero Paoletti.
1796 The 'meadow of the columns' is laid out.
c. 1834 The broad carriage drive is inaugurated. A large portion of the 17th century maze is transformed into *boschetti* in English landscape style.

Giardino Bardini
A marvelous surprise

HOW TO ARRIVE

Take the street that leads from
Ponte Vecchio to Forte Belvedere.
Address: Costa San Giorgio 1
and Via dei Bardi 1/r
Buses: 12, 23, C3, D
tel.: +39 055 2638599
+39 055 2346988 - +39 055 294883
E-mail: info@bardinipeyron.it
Visiting hours: Nov.-Feb.: 8:15 am -
4:30 pm; March: 8:15 am - 5:30 pm;
Apr.-May and Sept.-Oct.: 8:15 am -
6:30 pm; June-Aug.: 8:15 am - 7:30 pm.
Closed Jan. 1, May 1, December 25,
the first and last Monday of the month

The flower garden and the baroque stairway

To anyone walking up the Lungarno in the vicinity of Ponte alle Grazie, a splendid garden suddenly appears on Piazza Mozzi, beyond Palazzo Mozzi, occupying a site that was thickly overgrown with wild vegetation only a few years ago. At that time no one would have imagined that a hidden garden existed here.

Without a good knowledge of Florentine history it could hardly be thought, a few years ago, that those splendid trees, that corner of unspoiled nature wedged into the city, had been in the past one of Florence's most important gardens, where nature and art had struggled for supremacy.

Passing through the gate in the great wall opening onto Costa San Giorgio to enter this mysterious garden is an unforgettable experience. In ideally tracing the steps of the antiquarian Stefano Bardini, and then of his son Ugo, as they placed sculptures at strategic points, the visitor is struck by a wave of contrasting emotions. A striking view of the city, so near and yet so far, appears in a birds-eye view, so high are we and so close to almost touching those domes, spires, and walls. From here the gaze sweeps over one of Florence's most splendid panoramas.

The garden, laid out in the 1960s, was abandoned after the death of Ugo Bardini due to the complicated vicissitudes of his inheritance, finally resolved in the year 2000. Restoration has brought it back to life, clearly revealing its separate parts, the legacy of its complex, centuries-long history.

This is in fact a garden composed of three gardens. The agricultural part to the east consists of a great orchard traversed by a path bordered with *noisette* roses, ending in a pergola of wisteria and hy-

*From left:
detail of
the stairway*

*the sculptural
group of* Ceres
and Bacchus

drangeas that leads up to the Belvedere. From the Belvedere, visitors overlook the centre of the baroque stairway lined with vases and statues. To the west, a totally different garden appears. This section is the Anglo-Chinese park, built at the initiative of Jacques Louis Le Blanc in the early years of the 19th century.

This great garden, abounding in historic memories, of exceptional artistic and botanical importance, is a work of art whose lost identity has been resurrected through five long years of painstaking restoration.

Itinerary of visit

The entrance on Piazza dei Mozzi leads to the lower part of the garden. After passing a bed of box, clipped in curious Art Nouveau forms, continue up the gentle slope, leaving to the left the rooftops and terraces of Palazzo Mozzi. Note in particular the wall fountain with decorations made of different materials, an element remaining from the 18th-century decoration of the lawn behind the *palazzo*.

Continuing to the right, we come upon another broad shallow niche decorated with the Mozzi

coat of arms. The other wall supports the terrace reached by the baroque stairway above us. On the left side of this terrace is a great niche made of stone architectural elements, with a marble statue composed by Ugo Bardini of various found pieces. These high walls result from the transformation of the medieval kitchen gardens, replaced by the Bardini family with a new road connecting the lower part of the garden and Palazzo Mozzi with the villa overlooking Costa San Giorgio. From here, turning to the right on the gravel path, we arrive at the first terrace with its 18th-century grotto. On the first ramp of the stairway stand two statues in masonry called *Vertumno and Pomona*. Passing a great pergola of climbing roses, we enter the flower garden, bordered in colourful herbaceous plants, a contemporary version of the baroque **flower garden**. Climbing the last ramp of terracotta steps, we are confronted with the strikingly scenic effect of the central part of the baroque stairway, overflowing with roses and iris in bloom.

Continuing to the left, a straight path slopes up to the agricultural part of the garden, where numer-

**Agricultural
area**

Giardino Bardini

Ceres and Bacchus

English garden

Rustic grotto

Dragon canal

The dragon canal

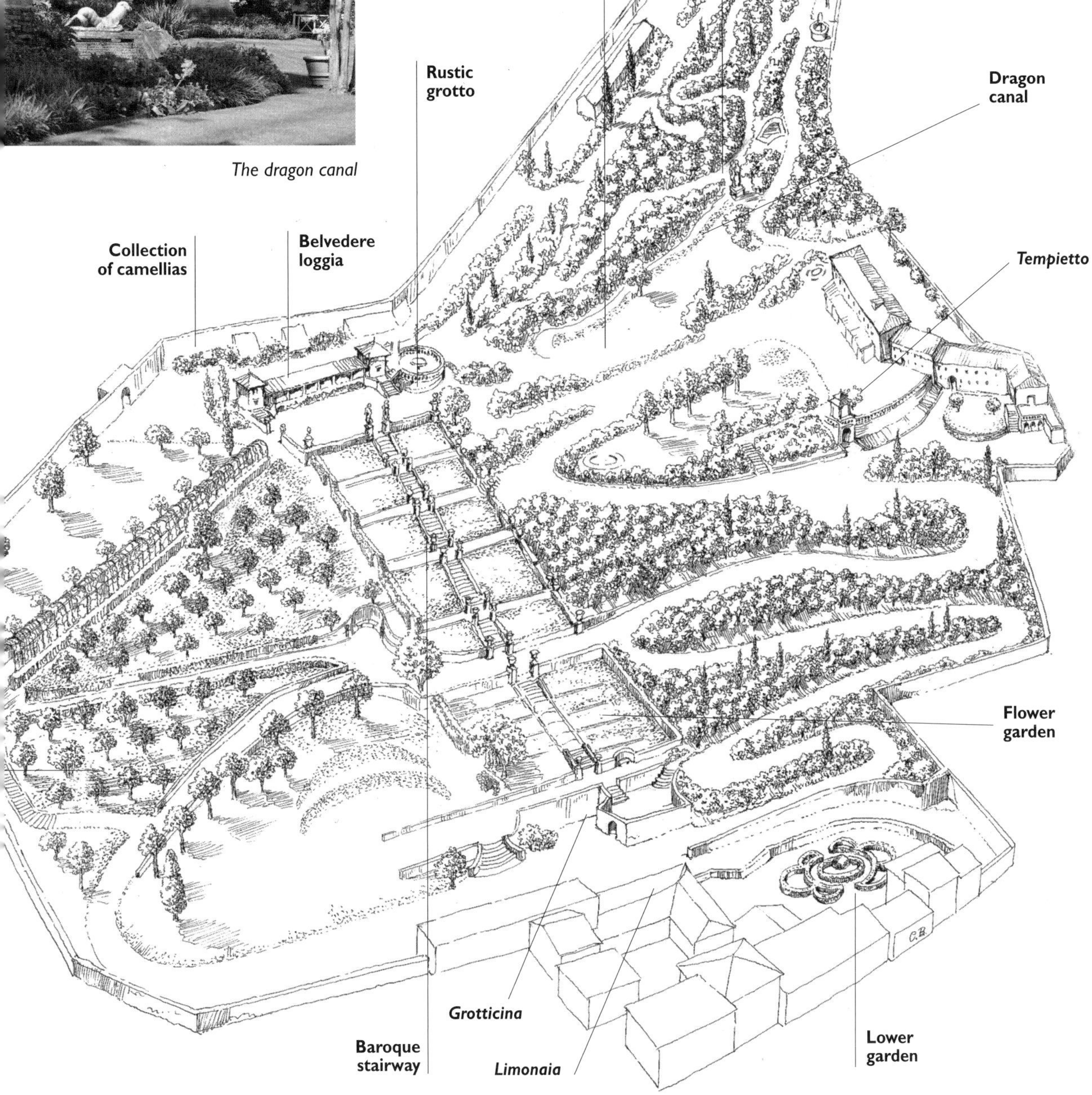

Collection of camellias

Belvedere loggia

Tempietto

Flower garden

Grotticina

Baroque stairway

Limonaia

Lower garden

ous varieties of ancient fruit trees have been planted, some of them trained 'espalier', others in dwarf form. We then pass through the high arched pergola of wisteria, embellished by the collection of hydrangeas, to arrive at the **Belvedere terrace**, now equipped with a coffee bar. From here we can admire a magnificent panorama over the city.

The wall on the west side of the stairway, which divided the Mozzi property from its neighbour, conserves important remains of its baroque features, with decorated panels and niches containing fountains that have been restored.

From here an intriguing path runs along the wall, where an important collection of camellias was planted some years ago. Here we can admire the great buttresses of the medieval walls, still displaying, in vicinity of Porta San Giorgio, corbels and arcades.

Returning to the Belvedere loggia, on the left we find a little rustic grotto remaining from the 19th-century furnishings of the Le Blanc garden.

Before us stands one of the most magnificent trees in the garden: an ancient yew that dominates and frames the panorama over Florence.

We then continue along the paths and meadows of the Le Blanc Anglo-Chinese garden up to the villa enlarged by Stefano Bardini. Noteworthy are some decorative elements remaining from the 19th-century waterworks, most notably the **dragon canal**, which has been restored and embellished by borders of shady herbaceous plants. Numerous garden furnishings were placed here by the antiquarian Bardini with great artistry and talent, to create scenes such as the **large sculptural group of *Ceres and Bacchus*** or the marble fountain (also composed of original elements with integrations) that marks the connection point between the stairway and the English landscape garden. Descending along the path toward the villa, we exit on Costa San Giorgio, pass through the ticket office and bookshop, and continue toward the Boboli Gardens.

To know more

M. Pozzana, *Guida del Giardino Bardini*, Florence 2005.

Cd-Rom: Fondazione Parchi Monumentali Bardini e Peyron, *Il giardino Bardini*, Florence 2001.

Web: www.bardinipeyron.it

The garden is managed by the Fondazione Parchi Monumentali Bardini e Peyron, promoted by the Ente Cassa di Risparmio di Firenze.

The Belvedere loggia

restoration of the garden

The garden theatre overlooking Florence

The Bardini Garden, closed and abandoned for over thirty years, has now been restored and is managed today by the Fondazione Parchi Monumentali Bardini-Peyron promoted by the Ente Cassa di Risparmio di Firenze. The goal of the restoration project was that of conserving and restoring the still existing elements in the garden of Stefano and Ugo Bardini. At the same time, restoration provided the chance to insert new elements in the garden, and most of all to enrich its botanical importance. Hence the great stairway has again become a flower garden as in the Baroque Age, with a flourishing collection of Bourbon roses bordered by reflowering iris. Overlooking the city, a garden theatre has been built for outdoor performances, two great orchards occupy grounds formerly used as farmland, and azaleas have come back to embellish the upper part of the English woods. A collection of camellias has been planted along the city wall; a great pergola covered with wisteria occupies the central part of the path leading up to the Belvedere, and below, sixty different hydrangeas form one of the garden's greatest botanical attractions.

Chronology

1309 The Comune of Florence decides to purchase the Mozzi property in the Popolo di S. Lucia de Magnoli. The estimation compiled mentions a palazzo 'with a great loggia and garden behind said palazzo and an adjacent house with vegetable garden and meadow, and walled land behind the house'.

Early 15th century Financial problems oblige the Mozzi to liquidate much of their property, including the family residence.

1551-1552 Luigi di Conte di Giovannozzo de Mozzi regains possession of part of the family residence. He also buys some orchards stretching over the hill of Montecuccoli, from the back of the palazzo as far as the walls. This area now constitutes the basic core of the Bardini garden's eastern section.

First half of the 17th c. The architect Gherardo Silvani (1579-1675) builds a villa in a panoramic position on Costa San Giorgio for Giovan Francesco Manadori. Annexed to the villa are some farmlands, including a vineyard that will become the first core of the western part of today's Bardini Garden.

1603 Piero di Luigi di Conte dei Mozzi consolidates ownership of the palazzo, by purchasing the remaining part from Ersilia della Gherardesca.

1781 The property is enlarged when a 'house with a large orchard' extending as far as the city walls is donated to Giulio Mozzi by Margherita D'Orford, who leaves him all of the property she owns (including Villa Medici at Fiesole).

1793 The villa Manadori, on Costa San Giorgio, is bought by the Cambiagi family.

1814 Giacomo Luigi Le Blanc, governor of the State of Piombino, is the owner of the house and the former Villa Manadori on Costa San Giorgio, along with all of the land around it, from Via de' Bardi to the walls. He spends lavishly to create in this area (today the western sector of the Bardini garden) a modern, for the time, English landscape park.

1839 Pier Giannozzo de Mozzi buys all of the western section of the park, bringing the property up to its present size and extension.

1880 Expropriation and sale at public auction of the property owned by Adolfo Mozzi del Garbo, the last of the Mozzi family.

1913 The antiquarian Stefano Bardini purchases the entire property. In spring of this same year, Bardini purchases from the City of Florence the ancient Customs Office annexed to the Porta. At his death the property is inherited by his son Ugo.

January 2000 Subsequent to an agreement between the Ministry of Finance and the Ente Cassa di Risparmio, restoration of the Bardini Garden begins.

October 2005 The garden is opened to the public

July 2007 The Villa is opened to the public.

Giardino Corsi (or Annalena)

Annalena

*The name of Annalena derives,
according to tradition,
from Anna Elena, daughter
of Galeotto Malatesta and wife
of Baccio d'Anghiari, killed
in a conspiracy plotted
by Cosimo the Elder.
Anna Elena, now a widow,
retired to monastic life,
founding a cloistered order
that was named Annalena
after her.*

The semicircular bench

Between the Torrigiani garden and the Boboli park is a small English garden, covering an area of barely half a hectare, filled with the surprises and artificial perspectives typical of the landscape fashion that swept Florence in the first half of the 19th century. The garden is distinguished by a broad elliptical bed with elaborate **parterres** of box and neoclassical elements. The words engraved on the marble plaques and stone bench emphasize the philosophical and contemplative atmosphere of the garden. Clipped hedges of laurel and viburnum and great trees – ilex, cedar and magnolia – envelop the visitor in a rarified atmosphere populated by terra-cotta statues, originally covered with stucco to imitate marble.

The origins of the garden date back to the 15th century, when the area formed part of an ancient orchard owned by the Annalena nuns. The present-day garden was however laid out between 1801 and 1810 by Giuseppe Manetti, commissioned to create it by Marchese Tommaso Corsi, who had recently become the owner of the property. In 1544, during the war against Siena, Cosimo I had ordered a line of fortifications to be built within the existing walls of Oltrarno. The area coinciding with the present-day garden was split in half by the line of bastions. When the new wall was demolished in 1571 the land remained abandoned, cluttered with an enormous pile of earth and bricks for over two centuries.

The property was still in this condition when Manetti started to create the new garden. One of the most brilliant and innovative landscape artists in Florence at that time, he utilized the huge mass of debris with great ingenuity to create a number of features culminating in the terrace facing on Via dei Serragli. By doing so he managed to transform the little space available into a fascinating garden, boasting a collection of plants that was famous among the botanists of the day.

Itinerary of visit

To establish an itinerary seems almost to contradict the intention of the designer who, in an area of restricted size, ingeniously created an atmosphere where the visitor can almost lose himself, forgetting that he is in the heart of the city. To best appreciate the garden, walk around the outer edge and observe the neo-classical entrance on Via Romana with the two images of dancing girls, the Loggetta del Canto (on the corner between Via Romana and Via del Moro), the statue of *Mercury* and the bass-relief with winged figures. These elements were carefully placed by Manetti to delimit the inner space and accentuate its isolation from the city. The *boschetto*, or small wooded area, visible above the wall that runs along Via dei Serragli, has a similar function. Once inside the garden, let yourself be guided by the feelings aroused by the vegetation and furnishing elements. Stroll along the path that winds through the trees; observe the terra-cotta statue in the laurustrine niche and pause to rest on the **semicircular bench** decorated with elegant neo-classical designs (the same designs appear on the facade of the villa). Near the elliptical bed on which the garden centers is a spacious aviary and further on, toward the boundary wall, appears the building of the *limonaia*. A stone inscription praises friendship and the words engraved on the stone bench remind the visitor that "the wise must submit to fate".

The central parterre

Giardino Torrigiani
A romantic park

HOW TO ARRIVE

In the immediate vicinity of Piazza Tasso, with entrance on the street that leads from Ponte alla Carraia to Porta Romana.
Owners: The Torrigiani di S. Cristina and Torrigiani Malaspina families
Address: Via de' Serragli 146
tel.: +39 055 224527
fax: +39 055 229662
Visiting hours: for groups, by appointment only
Restrooms

Sculptural group with lion attacking a bull

The Torrigiani garden, one of the largest gardens located within the walls (covering an area of seven hectares) is perhaps the most important romantic park in the city. This extraordinary creation fully expresses the aesthetic and philosophical ideal of the English garden, whose landscape model, in contrast to the architectural one of the Italian and French garden, developed in Europe during the 18th century and began to spread through Italy near the end of the century. The project by Luigi de Cambray Digny, a highly cultured architect of French origin, dates from 1813. The owner Pietro Torrigiani had decided to create a garden itinerary steeped in Masonic symbolism. This is alluded to by the statues of the sphinx and of *Osiris* and the numerous architectural structures scattered over the park, such as the tempietto of Arcadia or the Torrino, placed to mark the most significant points. But the Masonic symbols were to remain mysterious and hard to decipher. Not even the *Guida del giardino Torrigiani*, published in 1824, was able to explain their meanings. What is instead apparent today are the aesthetic principles, reflecting the art of the English landscape garden: elegantly designed winding paths, broad meadows where flocks of sheep once grazed, artificial hillocks that animate the composition, conferring on it variety and profundity, majestic woods of rare and precious trees, wich constitute an important collection.

Itinerary of visit

Visitors enter from the gate on Via dei Serragli. On the right the statue of *Osiris*, the Egyptian god of death and resurrection, holds up two tables bearing rules for visiting the garden. "Dogs are not allowed, nor are horses and carriages", we read. "Do not touch the flowers, plants, or minerals. No games allowed without special permission. Walk only on the paths". To the right of the entrance a column commemorates the work of the botanist Pietro Micheli. At the end of the avenue stands the remarkably elegant villa in neo-classical style. On each side of it are formal gardens. The one on the right, next to the great *limonaia*, is adorned with beautiful marble vases. The one on the left is situated beside the nursery with greenhouses for indoor plants. Strolling along the right-hand path we pass before a *boschetto* of bamboo and then arrive at the **tempietto** of Arcadia. Inside the *tempietto* is a **sculptural group** representing a lion attacking a bull. Continuing along the paths bounded by hedges of laurel and other evergreens we reach a broad **circular lawn** in front of the villa, also known as the

The circular lawn looking toward the Torrino

*Above:
the
tempietto
of Arcadia*

*Bottom:
the circular
lawn
and the villa*

'cavallerizza', since it was originally designed as a place to race horses. Furnished with benches, vases and statues, this lawn is the ancient core of the property.

At the center of the lawn is a statuary group of remarkable size. Sculpted by Pio Fedi in the 19th century, it portrays *Seneca pointing the way to the young Pietro Torrigiani*. On the Via del Campuccio side is a gymnasium. The semicircular back, in the form of a theater, and the end building with its elegant neo-classical lines, now used as a small apartment, can be seen. We go on to climb the hillock built of debris from the 16th century earth bastions that defended Florence in the war against Siena. From here there is fine view of the garden below. On the hillock are a Chinese balance (an exotic game), an aviary and the famous **Torrino**, created by the architect Gaetano Baccani and inspired by the heraldic emblem of the Torrigiani family.

It was used as astronomical observatory and library. In the lower part of the garden, on the left, an extraordinary centuries-old beech and other unusual trees testify to the exceptional botanical importance of the garden throughout the 19th century.

Turning toward the level ground we encounter first, on the right, a dry ditch (recalling the project, never carried out, for bringing abundant water to the garden); then, still on the right, tennis courts. A little further on are the splendid stables; near them, on the southern side, the **nursery greenhouses** and a great formal garden, recently restored.

To know more

M.P. Maresca, *Il giardino Torrigiani,* in "Arte dei Giardini. Storia e restauro", 1993, II, pp. 55-77.

Web: www.giardinotorrigiani.it

Chronology

1531 Raffaello Torrigiani purchases an orchard and two houses located on the southern side of Via del Campuccio. This was to be the original core of the garden.

1571 The bastioned front built in 1544 for the war against Siena is demolished. The 'casino Torrigiani' is built.

End of 16th c. The Dominican Friar Agostino del Riccio describes the garden, praising its abundance of vegetables, variety of citrus fruits and jasmines.

17th c. Carlo Torrigiani and Camilla Strozzi enlarge the *casino di delizie*.

1716 The illustrious botanist Pier Antonio Micheli creates a garden in which to experiment with growing rare plants.

1802-1817 Pietro Torrigiani extends the property. The architect Bernardo Fallani is commissioned to enlarge the *casino*.

1813 Torrigiani commissions Luigi de Cambray Digny to renovate the garden, but he abandons the project after only one year.

1819 The architect Gaetano Baccani is called to direct the works in the garden. He creates the neo-gothic tower, the imitation battlements on the Medicean bastions, the gymnasium, the aviary and several other *giochi*. In the same year the first inventory of the plants in the garden is published. It lists 13,000 plants in the ground and 5,500 in vases.

1841 The second catalogue of the plants grown in the garden is published, edited by Antonio Targioni Tozzetti.

Above: interior view of a greenhouse

At left: a statue in the garden

Giardino Corsini al Prato
The triumph of geometry

HOW TO ARRIVE

In the vicinity of Piazzale di Porta al Prato, not far from the Santa Maria Novella railway station.
Owner: Prince Corsini
Address: Via il Prato 58
Bus: 12
Tel.: +39 055 210564
Visiting hours: by appointment only from 9:00 am to 1:00 pm and from 3:00 pm to sunset, Saturday afternoon and Sunday excluded.
Accessible to the disabled

The garden looking toward the palace

The beauty of the Corsini garden, entirely concealed to the view by the facade of the palace on the Prato, is breathtaking. In spring the flowering of pink and red rockrose, lavender, roses, peonies and cherry trees shows this to be one of the rare Florentine historical gardens that is well preserved today. Elegant lemon urns and solemn marble statues contribute to the sober elegance of the whole.

The landscape designer Oliva di Collobiano is responsible for the recent selection of flowers and aromatic herbs planted in great variety in the beds. Bounded by hedges of box, they contain ancient examples of *Poncirus trifoliata*, a thorny species of citrus fruit used for particularly intricate hedges. The history of the garden began in 1591 when Alessandro Acciaiuoli, already the owner of a house famous for its garden, purchased the land and commissioned Bernardo Buontalenti to build a palace. The work was not finished due to financial difficulties, and the "large house begun and not finished, with a garden and a *ragnaia*" was sold in 1621 to Filippo di Lorenzo Corsini.

Filippo commissioned the architect Gherardo Silvani to finish the *casino di delizia*. The garden annexed to Palazzo Acciaiuoli was not very large, but was extended by purchasing adjacent land. Gherardo Silvani designed a layout with sophisticated geometric divisions of the design in the center.

Enlarged by Gaetano Baccani between 1834 and 1836, the *casino al Prato* became the residence of Neri Corsini, Marchese of Laiatico, and Eleonora Rinuccini.

The geometric parterre

Itinerary of visit

The garden is entered from the Prato, through the great doorway for carriages. The beauty of the **geometric *parterre*** with its box hedges, beds of flowers and aromatic herbs, strikes the visitor with wonder and delight. Along the sides of the *parterre* are two English *boschetti*, designed in romantic style and created in the early 19th century, distinguished by great ilex and laurel trees.

The ground is covered by a carpet of acanthus. It is probable that one of the two *boschetti* was created by transforming an ancient *ragnaia* of ilex trees.

Next we find the avenue along the sides of which Cardinal Neri Corsini (1685-1770) placed an important antiquarian collection of classical inscriptions and marbles. Perpendicular to the loggia, the avenue divides the central portion of the garden in half.

The statues, standing on tall bases, create a fine perspective effect, conferring greater depth on the view. At the end of the avenue are two perfectly conserved *limonaie*, containing ancient tools for the cultivation of citrus trees. In spring there is a splendid flowering of pink peonies in front of the *limonaia* on the left; and an equally beautiful flowering of ornamental cherry trees before the one on the right. Beyond the *limonaie* a door opens in the encircling wall onto Via della Scala. After having crossed a lawn where ancient linden trees stand we find on the left the wall that separates the garden from a broad meadow and fruit orchard. This is the part of the garden that most resembles open countryside. Its rural aspect reminds us that, in the original design, the garden was to be a place capable of uniting ornamentation and cultivation of the land, knowledge of the useful and art of the delightful.

il Prato

Porta al Prato in an early 20th century postcard

Already by the Middle Ages the Prato d'Ognissanti had assumed fundamental importance in defining the urban structure of Florence. It was not a city square or *piazza*, but rather a great unpaved area, kept as *prato*, or meadow, and used for games, performances and so on. In the frenetic traffic of the city it is hard to imagine today the ancient calm of the broad Prato.

In the 16th and 17th centuries fine palaces were built around the Prato, the most imposing of them Palazzo Corsini, which conceals behind its facade one of the richest and best conserved gardens in Florence.

Orti Oricellari
The grotto of Polyphemus

HOW TO ARRIVE

In the immediate vicinity
of the Santa Maria Novella
railway station.
Owner: Assicurazioni Generali /
Mr. and Mrs. Ridomi
Address: Via Orti Oricellari 9
Buses: 1, 2, 17, 29, 30
Tramway: line 1
Visiting hours: by appointment
at Assicurazioni Generali Administra-
tion tel.: +39 055 2670175
Accessible to the disabled
Restrooms
(The other half of the garden
owned by Mr. and Mrs. Ridomi,
with entrance on Via Bernardo
Rucellai, is now undergoing
restoration and open to students
conducting research for graduate
theses; for information telephone
+39 055 2302212).

place of academic debate. The garden was transformed; first dedicated to philosophic meditation it now became the place of amusement and delight. Bianca, the mistress of Francesco I de' Medici, en-

*The grotto
under the palace*

The city block between Via della Scala, Via Rucellai, Via Palazzuolo and Via degli Orti Oricellari encloses a part of what was one of the most complex and refined gardens in Florence.

Conceived as a place of philosophical *otia* by Bernardo Rucellai (from which the name) in the early 16th century, the garden became the meeting place for literary figures, humanists, philosophers and historians such as Machiavelli, Buondelmonti, Jacopo da Diacceto, and Luigi Alamanni. Near the end of the century the Orti Oricellari were purchased by Bianca Cappello, and parties and games took the

tertained her friends with perfidious tricks. Clelio Malespini reports that there was a hole dug in the ground, concealed by wooden boards covered with grass, which opened like a trapdoor to receive the shocked guests who fell in. Awaiting the unlucky ones at the bottom of the hole were thirty pages wearing devils' costumes. But this was the only unpleasant surprise. Later, having recovered from the shock, guests were welcomed to the *loggetta* by "beautiful girls, entirely nude under golden mantles, superbly adorned, which lightly and barely concealed their secret parts, covered with pearls, dia-

The statue of Polyphemus

monds, rubies and sapphires, and drenched in perfume from head to foot".

Redesigned by Alfonso Parigi and Ferdinando Tacca for Giovan Carlo de' Medici around the middle of the 17th century, the garden was transformed into a park in the second decade of the 19th century by Luigi de Cambray Digny, commissioned by Giuseppe Stiozzi Ridolfi. The architect inserted the existing elements of the 17th century garden into a larger, more complex design, inspired by the philosophical and progressive ideals of Masonry. The themes common to the romantic garden were thus developed in the Orti Oricellari.

Itinerary of visit

From gate on the Via degli Orti Oricellari the **statue of** *Polyphemus*, sculpted in plastered masonry by Antonio Novelli, a pupil of Giambologna, can be seen. The garden is divided into two properties, making it hard to understand the original project, in which the statue and the grotto of Polyphemus were placed one before the other. In the section nearest to Via della Scala the garden is dominated today by the statue of Homer's giant. In the other part of the garden a group of 17th century grottoes can be visited. The Grotto of *Polyphemus* (or *antro dei Venti*) is decorated with *spugne*; an artificial hillock was built to house it. In the Grotto of the Baths, decorated with calcareous concretions, are bucolic images now ruined by time and humidity. Beyond the balustrade that separates the beds of the Villino Cesaroni, facing on Via Rucellai, from the park can be glimpsed the neo-classical facade of the *Pantheon* by De Cambray Digny. Restored in the 1860s, the building contains tombs and relics of the illustrious men who frequented the garden. The 17th century **grotto** located below the palace is magnificent, with niches decorated with shells and calcareous *spugne*.

To know more

L.M. Bartoli, G. Contorni, *Gli Orti Oricellari a Firenze: un giardino, una città*, Florence 1991.

VV.AA., *Il gigante degli Orti Oricellari*, Rome 1993.

M. Pozzana, *Giardini di città*, Florence 1994, p. 77 and ff.

Chronology

1481-1489 Bernardo Rucellai and Nannina de' Medici, his wife, purchase land in the vicinity of Porta al Prato.
Early 16th c. A *casino di delizia* with garden is built, the beginning of the Orti Oricellari.
1573 The property is bought by Bianca Cappello.
1641-1657 The Orti Oricellari become the property of Giovan Carlo I de' Medici.
1670 Ferdinando Ridolfi purchases the property and commissions Pier Francesco Silvani to enlarge it.
Early 19th c. Giuseppe Stiozzi Ridolfi requests Luigi de Cambray Digny to design for him an English landscape park.
Last decade of the 19th c. The garden is divided into two parts. Ferdinando Cesaroni buys the western part and builds two houses with access from Via Rucellai.

Giardino Budini Gattai
A collection of camellias

HOW TO ARRIVE

Between Piazza San Marco
and Piazza SS. Annunziata,
behind the Accademia Gallery.
Owners: The Budini Gattai family
Address: Via de' Servi 51
Buses: 6, 31, 32
tel.: +39 055 210832
fax: +39 055 212080
Visiting hours:
by appointment only, for groups
of 8-10 persons.
Admission: 10,00 €
Accessible to the disabled
Restrooms

*The fountain
of* Venus

The best time to visit the garden is undoubtedly spring when, around the end of March, the **camellias blossom** in splendid profusion. This collection, one of the few remaining in Florence, boasts plants of ancient variety and remarkable size. Entering from the great doorway on Piazza SS. Annunziata the visitor passes through the half-shadow of a monumental *portico* into this little 16th century jewel set in the heart of Florence. Ugolino Grifoni, the secretary of Cosimo I, had chosen this strategic site on which to build his palace and had commissioned Bartolomeo Ammannati to design it. The famous sculptor and architect worked on it, starting in 1563, for over ten years, creating a geometric garden of modest size but abounding in significance and decoration. A fountain with the statues of *Jason with sea monsters and Venus*, described in 17th century texts, was the most striking feature of the garden, along with the espaliers of citrus trees and evergreens what marked off the space according to customary Florentine tradition.

In the 18th century the garden was enlarged, the fountain moved, and in its place was built a wall-fountain to hold the statue of *Venus*.

In the late 19th century the garden became the property of the Budini Gattai family and underwent further transformation, entirely losing its old geometric layout to assume a new romantic guise.

During the same period the singular **banana grove** (*boschetto*) was planted in a small, protected courtyard; here the trees have found an ideal microclimate.

The collection of camellias, which has now become a real *boschetto*, was then planted in front of the loggia opening onto the garden. It contains, among other varieties, the double-flowered *Callista*, the splendid *Mutabilis Traversii* bearing double flowers with white petals streaked and bordered in red, and the *Terzjana* developed in Milan in 1845 and named in honor of Marchesa Terzi.

On an axis with the loggia is the rustic decoration **fountain** with the **statue of *Venus*** and the marine creatures that originally adorned the 16th century fountain. At the lower left, built into the wall of the palazzo, is a stone recording the date when the work was completed: 1574.

The boschetto *of banana trees*

To know more

M. Pozzana, *Il giardino di palazzo Grifoni*, in "Bartolomeo Ammannati Scultore e Architetto, 1511-1592", edited by Niccolò Rosselli del Turco and Federica Salvi, Florence 1995, pp.155-160.

Web: www.palazzobudinigattai.it

The garden with its camellias looking toward the palazzo

Orto botanico
The 'Giardino dei Semplici'

HOW TO ARRIVE

In the immediate vicinity
of Piazza San Marco.
Address: Via Micheli 3
Buses: 1, 10, 11, 17
tel.: +39 055 2757402
fax: + 39 055 2346760
Visiting hours:
from Oct. 16 to Mar. 31 Sat.-Mon.
10:00 am - 5:00 pm / from Apr. 1
to Oct. 15 10:00 am - 7:00 pm,
Wednesday closed
Guided visit: by appointment; schools
Oct.-June; groups all year round.
Admission: 6,00 €, reduced 3,00 €
(children 6-14); free admission
for over 65 and students (only of the
University of Florence)

The central fountain

Created around the middle of the 16th century, the Florentine Orto Botanico is a garden of great interest. Although conceived with scientific intentions, it was created according to the same principles of beauty, variety and elegance deemed valid for any other garden designed in the same period. It is a garden of knowledge, where the plants must be observed, a garden linked to the university world; but at the same time it is a place of wonder and delight.

It was the idea of Luca Ghini, famous physician and naturalist, professor at the University of Bologna, to let students enrolled in the faculty of Medicine study live medicinal plants. From Ghini's idea originated the first Botanical Garden, in Pisa. In 1545, at the recommendation of Ghini himself, Cosimo I decided that Florence too should have a botanical garden open to students of medical botany. From this decision came the *Giardino dei Semplici*, the third oldest of its kind, after the botanical gardens of Pisa (1543) and Padova (1545).

The project was commissioned of Niccolò Pericoli known as Tribolo, who proposed an irregular rectangular layout with an octagonal island at the center. The island was to be adorned by a marble fountain and surrounded by a moat crossed by mobile bridges. Starting from the island eight paths originally subdivided the garden into eight spaces of more or less triangular shape. The triangular sections were in turn divided into elegant geometric sections of small size, each of which contains varieties of plants to be studied. At the four sides of the garden are small *boschetti*.

Itinerary of visit

The layout of the garden today is quite different from the original plan, although the spatial organization into 'squares' divided by two broad crossing avenues, centered around a **fountain**, has been retained. The shape of the 'squares' and the secondary paths derives instead from transformations dating from the middle of the 18th century. The garden now has the shape of an irregular polygon. During the 19th century the garden was extended on the east-

Springtime flowering

tion of orchids. The large **greenhouses built of masonry** contain the most important collections in the Orto, including rare and exotic plants: **cicas, cactuses, and ferns**. In the northeast corner is the pond. On the Via La Pira side are long, narrow beds containing the rich collection of **medicinal plants**. In the opposite corner is an artificial hillock with ponds for aquatic plants. The rectangle of added land, which looks on Via Capponi, houses numerous conifers, including interesting examples of bald cypress (*Taxodium distichum*) with grotesque pneumatophores, above-ground roots emerging from the water through which the trees absorb oxygen. The various sections of the garden are occupied by trees, some of them centuries old, and by numerous shrubs and herbaceous plants, each identified the botanical scientific name.

A visit is particularly pleasant in spring, when the splendid collection of azaleas standing along the main paths is in full flower.

To know more

P. Luzzi, F. Fabbri, *I tre orti botanici di Firenze*, in "I Giardini dei Semplici e gli Orti botanici della Toscana", edited by S. Ferri e F. Vannozzi, Perugia 1993.

Web: www.msn.unifi.it

ern side, toward Via Capponi. From the entrance on Via Micheli (the original entrance was on today's Via La Pira) visitors accede to the eastern side of the garden to find themselves in front of glass greenhouses, the so-called *stufini*, which house a fine collec-

Chronology

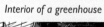

Interior of a greenhouse

1545 Cosimo I de' Medici rents land from the nuns of the Convent of San Domenico del Maglio. The Orto Botanico of San Marco is created.
1662 The first catalogue of the plants grown in the Orto is published.
1718 Cosimo III appoints the illustrious botanist Pier Antonio Micheli director of the garden.
1783 The Orto is assigned to the Accademia dei Georgofili.

1801 Management of the Orto is entrusted to Ottaviano Targioni Tozzetti, who orients the garden's collections toward botanical studies again.
19th c. The garden is extended toward Via Capponi and heated greenhouses are built.
Early 20th c. The library and collections of 'La Specola' museum of natural history are transferred here.
1929 The Orto becomes a public garden.

Il giardino del Museo archeologico
The fascination of ruins

HOW TO ARRIVE

In the vicinity of Piazza
SS. Annunziata.
Address: Via della Colonna 38
Buses: 6, 31, 32
tel.: +39 055 235750
+39 055 2480636
Visiting hours: Saturday 9:30 am-
12:30 pm, guided visits every 45
minutes
Admission: 4,00 €, reduced
2,00 € (18-25 years old): free
admission for under 18 and
over 65
Accessible to the disabled
Restrooms and bookshop

Tomb of Casale Marittimo

The garden of the Archaeological Museum is a narrow rectangular plot where flowers and colors are concentrated to form a kind of barrier against the pressure of the city. This is the garden of the Crocetta Palace, transformed in the early 20th century into an original collection of archaeological monuments of various provenance which, according to the ambitious project of Luigi Adriano Milani, were reconstructed in the garden and inserted into a new context. The history of the garden began when Lorenzo the Magnificent purchased several houses in the area, planning to build a colossal urban villa surrounded by gardens. The project, which was to have been directed by Giuliano da Sangallo, was never carried out because the nearness of the Ospedale degli Innocenti and three other important religious structures, the Crocetta Monastery, the Angiolini Monastery and the Church of Santissima Annunziata made the place more suitable to religious retreat than to the construction of *casini di delizia*. When Cosimo II decided to enlarge the building, the garden was, in fact, adapted to the usage imposed by a cloistered life. The side walls were raised and the neighboring houses lowered to ensure maximum privacy to occupants of the garden. At the end of the garden a small chapel was then built. In the first half of the 18th century the Prince of Craon rearranged the space bounded by the walls and Francesco Romoli, the Boboli gardener, created twelve **parterres** cultivated to citrus trees and vineyards, in the most classic tradition of Medicean gardens. A large room for citrus trees was also built. The layout with rectangular beds survived up the 19th century, when it was changed by the introduction of a circular element that transformed the two quadrangular sections nearest the palace. After having temporarily housed the Court of Accounts at the time when Florence was capital of Italy, the Crocetta Palace was chosen in 1879 as the site of an Archeological Museum in which ancient sculptures coming from the Uffizi and various villas would be placed. After the failure of several projects of this kind, Luigi Adriano Milani proceeded to create a garden closely linked to the museum, in which to place sculptures and architectural monuments coming from archaeological excavations. From 1900 to 1903, assisted by the architect Giuseppe Castellucci, Milani reconstructed a number of Etruscan tombs in the garden. This project, linked to other interesting experiments in the outdoor exhibition of archaeological material, has the merit of providing Florence with a museum itinerary inserted in a garden, important in spite of its small size.

Tomb of the Crucifix of Tufo

The ancient yew tree

Itinerary of visit

From the loggia of the palace, today the site of both the Archaeological Museum and the Department of Archaeology, visitors enter the garden. The circular pond survives from the original layout. On the right we find the tomb of the Diavolino (7th c. BC) coming from Vetulonia, reconstructed in 1901-1902, and another tomb from Vetulonia with an inscription bearing the name of the deceased carved on the lintel. On the left is the tomb of Tlesnei, with barrel ceiling, reconstructed in 1899. Further on, to the right, is the Inghirami tomb, a faithful copy of

the tomb discovered at Volterra in 1861 containing 53 alabaster funerary urns. Before the tomb stands a majestic **centuries-old yew tree** with thick green foliage. Dispersed among the vegetation and the bright colors of the seasonal flowers are the tomb of Veio (7th c. BC) and the **tomb of Casale Marittimo**, with circular cell; before the latter is the so-called 'lion of Tuscania'. Near the tempietto is the **tomb of the Crucifix of Tufo**, the altar and *favissa* (votive grave) from Bolsena. In the western part of the garden are two modern greenhouses.

To know more
Il giardino del Museo archeologico nazionale di Firenze, edited by Antonella Romualdi, Florence 2000.

flowers
in the
Baroque
garden

The tulip arrived in Europe in the mid-16th century. The vogue for collecting flower bulbs swept through European gardens in the following centuries, when garden owners were infected by the so-called 'tulip craze' of the times.

Donated by a German diplomat to the botanist Carlo Clusio around 1570, the tulip became the most precious flower bulb in the Netherlands within a few years. Expert hybridizing soon produced varieties grown with petals of various shape – pointed or fringed, 'parrot's crest' or double, multicolored or streaked. The tulip was not alone to populate 17th century gardens; numerous other bulbs were ardently sought after and collected. Their fascination can be felt again in looking at the miniatures by Giovanna Garzoni, commissioned by Cardinal Giovan Carlo de' Medici. They are splendid 'portraits' of flowers meticulously described and perfectly recognizable, displayed in splendid vases, either glass or blue-and-white Chinese porcelain. Nothing more than Garzoni's miniatures gives an idea of how splendid the flowering season must have been, at the time, in the garden of the Orti Oricellari. We are shown anemones in full flower and coronary anemones, fritillaries, hyacinths, narcissus tazzetta, narcissus 'of the poets', and narcissus pseudonarcissus (buttercups), tulips in great variety, with the predomination of 'parrot' tulips.

All of the Medicean gardens boasted flowers that sometimes cost a fortune. During the 18th century bulbous flowers were superseded by herbaceous plants. The flowering of the former, although magnificent, lasts in fact only a very brief time.

Flowering of **Narcissus tazetta**

camellias

The camellia, known also by the name 'Japanese rose' is an evergreen shrub with beautiful dark green glossy leaves, which may reach the size of a tree. Its scientific name is *Camellia japonica* and the plant belongs to the family of the *Theaceae*. Tea is in fact made from the leaves of a particular variety of camellia, the *Camellia sinensis*.

The first camellia introduced into Italy was the 'Celebratissima'; it was cultivated in the Reggia of Caserta around 1760. In the late 18th and early 19th centuries the camellia spread throughout central and northern Italy. There were numerous camellia collectors in Florence in the 19th century; during this same period camellias were also very popular in the area around Lucca.

Camellias in a garden near Pistoia

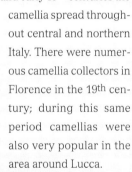

The cammelia flower can have innumerable magnificent shades of color, from pure white to pink to red, with a great variety of stripes, spots and dotting. The multifold shapes are classified under three headings: simple flowers, semi-double (with corolla irregularly imbricated, that is petals arranged without order in the form of an anemone or that of a peony),

Camellia japonica
semi-double marbled

double (they may be irregular, star-shaped or spiraling). There is a wide range of sizes, from 6.5 cm to about 13 cm in some varieties grown today. The plants usually flower in springtime, although the royal *Camellia sasanqua* blossoms in all its splendor in autumn. For some years now, thanks to the exhibitions held at Pieve di Compito, in the Lucchesia, and in the Budini Gattai garden in Florence, the camellia has returned to attract the interest of flower-lovers; numerous varieties are again being cultivated. In the vicinity of Villa Borrini, famous for its splendid camellia garden, the Borrini nursery at Sant'Andrea di Compito, in the Lucchesia, produces a remarkable number of varieties, as does the Tesi nursery at Pistoia. The *boschetto* of camellias at Villa Mansi in the Lucchesia displays the varieties *Camellia japonica* 'Lefevriana'(1841), *Camellia japonica* 'Carlotta Papudoff' (1861) and *Camellia japonica* 'Giuseppina Mercatelli' (1880). At Villa Torrigiani are splendid examples of *Camellia japonica* 'Fimbriata' (1816) and *Camellia japonica* 'Imbricata alba'. Again at Florence, in the Budini Gattai garden, we find the double-flowered *Callista*, the splendid *Mutabilis Traversii* bearing double flowers with white petals streaked and bordered in red and the *Terzjana*, created at Milan in 1845 and dedicated to Marchesa Terzi.

To know more
G. Cattolica, A. Lippi, P.E. Tomei, *Camelie dell'Ottocento in Italia*, Lucca 1992.

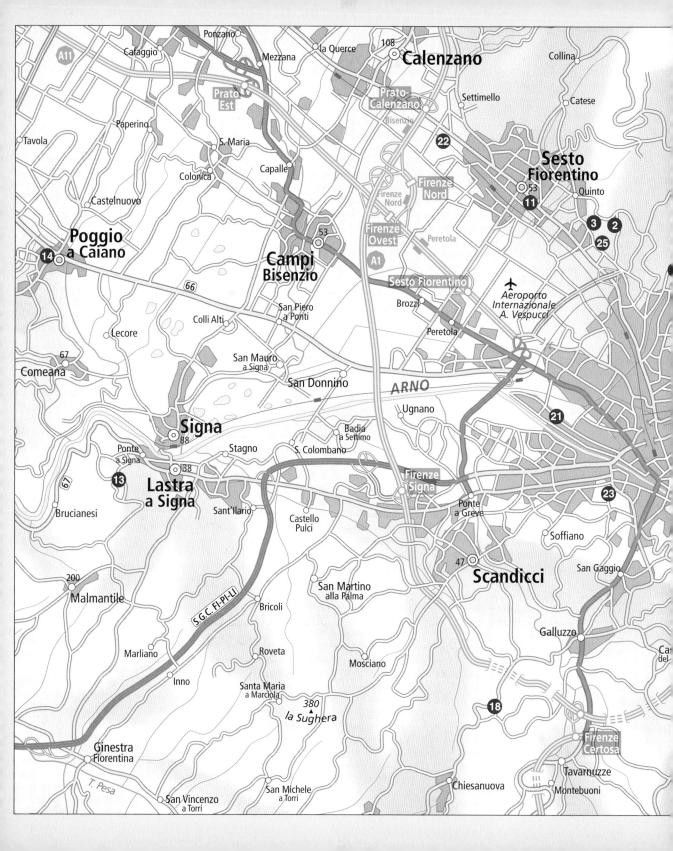

Florence
outside the walls

1	Giardino Capponi	44
2	Villa della Petraia	48
3	Giardino di Castello	52
4	Villa La Pietra	58
5	Villa Gamberaia	60
6	Villa La Quiete	66
7	Le Balze	68
8	Villa I Tatti	70
9	Fonte Lucente	72
10	Villa Medici	76
11	Villa Corsi Salviati	78
12	Pratolino	82
13	Villa di Bellosguardo	88
14	Poggio a Caiano	90
15	Villa Casagrande	92
16	Giardino dell'Iris	94
17	Giardino dell'Orticoltura	94
18	I Collazzi	94
19	Palazzo Medici Riccardi	94
20	Palazzo Vivarelli Colonna	94
21	Parco delle Cascine	94
22	Parco del Neto	94
23	Parco Strozzi al Boschetto	94
24	Villa di Careggi	94
25	Villa Corsini a Castello	95
26	Villa Schifanoia	95
27	Villa Stibbert	95
28	Villa Il Ventaglio	95

Giardino Capponi
The most beautiful view of Florence

HOW TO ARRIVE

In the vicinity of Piazzale
Michelangelo, near the Arcetri
astronomical observatory.
Owner: Maria Teresa Benedetti
Address: Via del Pian dei Giullari 3
Bus: 11
tel.: +39 055 2298609
fax: +39 055 223465
Visiting hours: upon presentation of
request in writing and only for groups
of at least 10 persons
Guided visits
Partially accessible to the disabled
Restrooms

the house and bounded by walls with fine scroll decorations.

The different areas have been created at different times: the secret garden, located below the terraced level on which stands the villa, was laid out in the late 16th century, probably by the owner Gino Capponi.

*The lawn
in front of the villa*

The rear facade of the villa extends in its severe elegance along the road front. Villa Capponi has always exerted a special fascination over the visitor, transmitting a sense of calm solemnity, perhaps impossible to achieve today in designing a garden. Contributing to the remarkable effect of the whole are the perfect proportions of garden and villa, the balance between closed and open spaces, the fluid communication between the different levels, between countryside and house.

The garden is composed of a great **lawn** in front of the house and three smaller levels, in reality three outdoor rooms: the lemon garden, the secret garden, and the rose garden, skillfully laid out around

It links in emblematic manner the different levels of the house in its higher position and the countryside below. At the same time connections between the different levels are ingeniously created by an underground passage that leads from the semi-basement level to the **secret garden**.

The citrus garden was created later, in 1774, by Ferdinando Carlo Capponi, who demolished a portion of the *selvatico*, or wilderness, and planted 1,600 small box bushes. In the 19th century the garden underwent no major changes. In 1882, when the property was bought by Lady Scott of Ancrum, the villa probably had the appearance of a neglected jewel. Although it had lost its economic importance

The secret garden

as a small farm it was fascinating to the eyes of its new owner. Lady Scott added the second walled garden below the secret garden, linking them by a stairway in masonry. This rose garden reiterates the ornamental theme of the walls in the upper garden, but also utilizes tall cypress hedges clipped in topiary shapes to make the composition more striking. Lady Scott also made changes in the facades of the villa, adding the two loggias and, presumably, closing the semi-underground corridor and transforming it into a rustic grotto.

The garden continued to evolve. Henry Clifford, who bought the villa in 1928, commissioned the English landscape artist Cecil Pinsent to design a swimming pool for the lower part of the garden. The new initiative did not change the existing aspect, since Pinsent decided to surround the pool with high cypress hedges, and to place stone statues around it.

A new outdoor room was thus created, ensuring privacy for swimming and sunbathing. Pinsent completed the vegetation along the country road beneath the terraced lawn in front of the house. He may also have designed the topiaries standing against the front facade of the villa and the others placed before the window in the secret garden.

Itinerary of visit

From Via del Pian dei Giullari we enter the half-shad-

Above:
the lawn in front of the villa,
with a view of Florence

Bottom:
a statue beside
Pinsent's swimming pool

ow of the doorway giving on the lawn. A stone gate opens onto the path that ideally extends into the countryside below. The roadway, little more than a path that runs along the wall of the terraced lawn, is bounded by hedges of lilac and bordered with iris.

The stone portal is dominated by two terra-cotta griffons. At the sides, slightly recessed, two *terra-cotta* lions bear a coat of arms. Beyond the portal, to the right, we enter the **lemon garden**, encircled by decorated walls, where flowerbeds of myosotis bordered with box surround the potted citrus trees. In line with the entrance portal, against the back wall, is a stone basin. On the right, behind the straight wall, stand cypresses and ilexes, what remains today of the original *selvatico* demolished in the 1770s to make room for the new garden.

The garden is canonically divided into four sections, each of them further subdivided into beds of box embellished by magnificent lemon urns.

Returning to the lawn, we continue up to border of the terrace overlooking the secret garden. From here there is an unforgettable view of the city.

We then descend a stairway to find the enclosed, intimate space of the flower garden with its abundant blossoming of silene. Behind us is the little grotto,

The lemon garden

or *grotticino*, created in the late 19ᵗʰ century by closing the ancient semi-underground corridor that leads to the kitchen. Nearby is a small stone pool used to irrigate the garden. The rectangular space is surrounded on all four sides by decorated walls. A window opens out in the west wall, giving a view of Pian dei Giullari.

Through a portal with iron gate we descend to the lower garden, or rose garden. Tall cypress hedges form walls of vegetation rising almost as high as the outer walls. Before a great semi-circular hedge of yew are three stone benches.

We then go down through the entrance lined with cypress hedges to find **Pinsent's swimming pool**. Inspired by Renaissance pools and fountains, it reiterates the theme of the mascaron spraying a jet of water, as well as the decoration scheme with **statues** and benches placed in alternation along walls of vegetation.

Following the charming rural path we go back up toward the stairway leading to the terraced lawn.

In the early years of the century, perhaps at the initiative of Pinsent himself, cypresses and box hedges clipped in spherical shape were planted along the paths that lead from the garden into the countryside.

To know more

M. Pozzana, *Una guida per conoscere Villa Capponi*, Florence 2000.

Cecil Pinsent's swimming pool

Chronology

1568-1572 Gino di Lodovico Capponi and his wife Maddalena Benci purchase property situated in the Popolo of San Leonardo in Arcetri. The first core of Villa Capponi is built, then enlarged and embellished with a garden.

1765 Ferdinando Carlo Capponi inherits the villa and makes sweeping changes.

1882 The Capponi family sell the villa to Lady Scott. She creates the third secret garden, conceiving of it as a particular *rose garden*. She also adds to the villa loggias built with sandstone columns coming from the demolition of the *Mercato Vecchio* (Old Market) of Florence.

1928 The villa is bought by Henry and Esther Clifford. Henry Clifford, curator of the painting section of the Philadelphia Museum of Art, has met Cecil Pinsent through his friend Bernard Berenson, and commissions him to design the swimming pool, finished in 1930.

1978 The Cliffords sell the villa to its present owners.

Villa della Petraia
The garden of fruits

cerned with details to the point of inserting some imaginary ones, he shows us more clearly than any other source how the garden was constructed. Beside the villa was the little orchard of '*frutti nani*' or dwarf fruit trees. On the level below was the flower

HOW TO ARRIVE

Between Sesto Fiorentino and Careggi, in the vicinity of Quinto.
Address: Via di Petraia 40, Castello
Bus: 2, 18, 28
tel.: +39 055 452691 / 055 451208
fax: +39 055 452691
Visiting hours:
June-Aug.: 8:15 am -6:30 pm
Sept.-Oct. and Apr.-May: 8:15 am - 5:30 pm
Nov.-Feb.: 8:15 am -3:30 pm
March: 8:15 am - 4.30 pm.
Closed the 2nd and 3rd Monday of the month
Free admission - Guided visits
Restrooms
Vending machine for snack and coffee

The lower parterre

Despite the great changes undergone by the Petraia garden, its aspect today is very close to the original one. The garden was laid out in the 16th century over three terraces, the one on the same level as the villa (now known as the **piano della Figurina** from Giambologna's statue of *Venus* that adorns the fountain); the intermediate terrace, with the nursery and flower garden; and the lower terrace, originally a fruit orchard distinguished by two great circular beds. A very clear picture of the garden as it appeared in the late 16th century can be seen in the lunette by Justus Utens depicting the villa with its garden. Although the painter was con-

garden with potted citrus trees. On the third level was the great *fruttiera*, or garden of fruit trees, with *boschetti* and *cerchiate* of ilexes bounding the two flowerbeds. The projects carried out during the course of the 19th century have altered this design in favor of a formal solution appearing today as an elliptical layout with little flowerbeds in the upper part. The park behind the garden is an important example of Central European landscaping style. Winding paths meander through thick vegetation (fine conifers grow here) with ample views opening onto flowery meadows, a sea of jonquils in Springtime and lovely scenes of the surrounding landscape.

Itinerary of visit

From the gate on Via della Petraia a broad avenue slopes upward to the side entrance, leading directly to the lower terrace through a *boschetto* of ilexes. Next comes a spacious **parterre** sloping gently downhill, divided into beds now planted to dwarf pear trees. Further on are geometric flower beds of elaborate design, providing a fine example of the 19th century flower garden.

Below a great avenue of plane trees bounds the southern side of the garden, while in the center a fountain emphasizes the central axis of symmetry along which the garden is laid out. A stairway leads to the intermediate level where a rectangular basin

A topiary against the wall around the 'piano della Figurina'

The 'piano della Figurina'

A hillside covered with villas

Villa Petraia is situated
on the slopes of
Monte Morello, in a sunny,
panoramic position.
In the 16th century, at the
time when villas first began
to be built on these hills, the
geometry of the agricultural
fields divided into plots
by the Romans many
centuries before could still
be seen. The numerous villas
that still today populate
the hillside, from the Villa
of Castello to the nearby
Villa Corsini, from Villa
La Quiete to the many
private villas all around,
testify to the love
of the Medici and other
Florentine families linked
to the Grand Ducal court
for this beautiful hillside.

*The fountain of Fiorenza
and the villa*

The flower garden

The fishpond

holds water used for irrigation. On the left a **flower garden**, recently recreated, revives the 17th century fashion for flower bulbs and what has been called the 'tulip craze' of the times.

Ideally, the garden should be visited in springtime to appreciate the splendid flowering of fritillaries, antique and 19th century varieties of tulips and 'Grand-ducal' hyacinths.

Chronology

1568 Ferdinando de' Medici begins the work of transforming the villa and garden.

1573-1574 The terraced levels of the garden are constructed.

1588 Grand Duke from 1587, Ferdinando commissions Raffaello di Zanobi di Pagno to resume work on the garden and villa.

1609 La Petraia passes to Ferdinando's son, Don Lorenzo.

1785-1788 The fountain of Fiorenza, built by Tribolo and adorned with a small bronze statue by Giambologna, is moved to the villa from the garden of Castello.

1798-1813 In the years of Napoleonic domination the lower garden is redesigned with a fountain at the centre.

1829 Leopoldo II (1824-1859) begins constructing the great English landscape park, designed by Joseph Frietsch.

1872 The Belvedere is built. The *piano della Figurina* is renovated to the design of Ferdinando Lasinio. The estate, become Savoia property subsequent to the unification of Italy, is the favorite residence of Vittorio Emanuele II and the *bella Rosina*, his beloved.

Climb the central stairway again to reach, above the **nursery**, the level of the villa. On the right can be seen copies of Tribolo's marble fountain with the bronze statue of *Fiorenza* or *Venus* by Giambologna (the original, which was brought here from the Villa of Castello, is on the first floor of the Villa of Petraia. The marble fountain is now being restored in an adjacent building).

The circular flowerbeds have recently been replanted according to the model of the 'bread basket' flower bed. To the left of the villa is a little woods with fine cedar trees, planted under the reign of the Savoia. Behind the villa an unusual fountain is formed of a great calcareous *spugna*. The path on the right leads to the 19th century park, the one on the left to the Villa of Castello.

To know more

C. Acidini, G. Galletti, *Le Ville e i Giardini di Petraia e Castello*, Pisa 1992.

Web: www.uffizi.firenze.it/musei/petraia

Giardino di Castello
Nature, science and beauty

HOW TO ARRIVE

Between Sesto Fiorentino and
Careggi.
Address: Via di Castello 44, Castello
Bus: 2, 18, 28
tel.: +39 055 454791
+39 055 451208
fax: +39 055 452691
Visiting hours:
June-Aug.: 8:15 am - 7:00 pm
Sept.-Oct. and Apr.-May:
8:15 am - 6:00 pm
Nov.-Feb.: 8:15 am - 4:00 pm
March: 8:15 am - 5.00 pm.
Closed the 2nd and 3rd Monday
of the month
Free admission
Accessible to the disabled
Restrooms

A splendid white azalea in front of the Grotto of the Animals

Castello is the first of the Medicean gardens in order of time, and is perhaps the most fascinating for its magnificence. Between 1537 and 1538 Cosimo I decided to enlarge and improve an estate that had been owned by his family since 1477. Niccolò Pericoli known as Tribolo was chosen to lay out the garden, according to a densely symbolic plan. Built around a central maze of cypresses on a line with the *Grotto of the Animals*, the garden was designed as an allegory of Medicean good government. Castello was known as a garden of statues, which numerous artists were called upon to deco-

rate; in addition to Tribolo, Pierino da Vinci, Bartolomeo Ammannati and Giambologna, all of whom remarkably embellished the garden by creating its famous grotto.

In narrating the life of Tribolo, Giorgio Vasari describes the garden of Castello and the complex iconological program traditionally attributed to Benedetto Varchi, a program designed to celebrate the Grand Duchy of Cosimo I as a true golden age. Tribolo was also responsible for the concept of the *Grotto of the Animals*, on which other artists, including Vasari, worked after his death. The most consistent changes, apart from the 18th century enlargement of the citrus tree rooms, were made in the 1770s and '80s, when the maze was demolished, the fountain of *Fiorenza* removed (and brought to Petraia) and the entire design of the central portion of the garden was altered. The fountain of *Fiorenza* was replaced by the one with the sculptural group of *Hercules strangling Antaeus* by Ammannati. Later on Leopoldo II created the great English parks of Castello and Petraia and the avenue linking the two villas.

Itinerary of visit

The avenue in front of the villa results from successive transformations of the original one, considered one of the wonders of the villa. It was formed of the great *cerchiata* of mulberry trees that Tribolo had designed to link the villa, in a bold landscaping initia-

tive, to the Arno River. Access to the garden is found to the left of the main entrance to the villa, now the headquarters of the Accademia della Crusca. The garden appears as an ample walled orchard divided into geometric compartments, and is dominated by the fountain with the statue of *Hercules strangling Antaeus*, surrounded by other marble statues. In springtime great vases of azaleas are placed round the fountain; at its sides are flowerbeds bounded by hedges of box. In spring the flowerbeds are splendid with antique roses, peonies and bulbs. Next comes the lemon garden, recently replanted with citruses in the ground, to be protected in winter according to the tradition of Medicean gardens. On the left are two huge *limonaie*, where the renowned collection of potted citrus trees, numbering over 500,

The garden of Castello

the Grotto
of the Animals

From the lemon garden the grotto is entered through a classical portal adorned with columns and pilaster strips, dating from the late 18th century. The grotto is composed of two chambers. The first is covered by a ceiling richly decorated with mascarons and festoons made of shells and marble *tesserae*. At the sides are two splendid marble basins decorated with marine animals and surmounted by groups of terrestrial animals that seem to emerge from the rock. The second, smaller, chamber has a barrel ceiling with incrustations of *pietra spugna* and a basin surmounted by a third group of animals dominated by the figure of a unicorn, a

symbolic animal deemed to possess the power of purifying water. This then was the message that the grotto was designed to express: purified water falls from the plaited hair of *Fiorenza*-Florence, to symbolize, placed inside the maze, the creation of a Medicean Garden of Eden. It should also be remembered that the originality of the composition, the precious materials and the striking impression they aroused were surely intensified by the presence of water spouting from the floor and flowing copiously from the ceiling. Many artists worked on the grotto, among them Tribolo and Vasari, who may have modified Tribolo's project; Francesco Ubertini known as Bachiacca, probably responsible for the magnificent basins with festoons of fish and seashells; Bartolomeo Ammannati, who sculpted some of the animals in bronze in 1558; and Giambologna, who created the bronze animals now in the Bargello.

is kept in winter. Go on from here to the **Grotto of the Animals**, excavated in the embankment above which has been planted a *selvatico* (see description of the grotto). To the right of the grotto a stairway leads to the upper level, from which the fountain of the *Apennine* by Ammannati, dated 1563, can be admired. Lower down on the eastern side is an entrance leading to the little walled garden known as the *ortaccio*. This garden, echoing the tradition of the Renaissance herb garden, contains a recent collection of aromatic plants. Still on the eastern side is the *stufa dei mugherini*, the warm greenhouse planned by Cosimo III for the cultivation of the delicate Goa jasmine, known as 'the Grand Duke's jasmine' (*Jasminum sambac*).

In recent years the garden has been enriched by a fine collection of azaleas, displayed at various points during the blossoming season. Standing against the walls enclosing the garden are espaliers of grape vines and fruit trees with borders of iris at their feet. Another botanical curiosity is represented by some dwarf pear trees, at the center of the flowerbeds in the lower *parterre*, recalling the traditional form of Renaissance cultivation. In the flowerbeds peonies, spring bulbs and antique roses blossom splendidly in season.

To know more

C. Acidini, G. Galletti, *Le Ville e i Giardini di Petraia e Castello*, Pisa 1992.

G. and S. Tintori, *Gli agrumi ornamentali. Consigli dalla tradizione dei contadini giardinieri,* with an articole by Paolo Galeotti, Bologna/Milan/Rome 2000.

S. Casciu, M. Pozzana, *Ville e giardini nei dintorni di Firenze*, Florence 2010.

Web: www.uffizi.firenze.it/musei/villacastello

the lunette
by Justus Utens

In 1599, when Justus Utens depicted the villa, the garden had been completed. The painter's lunette gives a precise picture of the estate. Before the villa is the great lawn with fish-ponds; at the sides of the building, the flower gardens. The first fountain, with the statue of *Hercules strangling Antaeus* by Ammannati, is followed by the cypress maze; within it stands the statue of *Fiorenza* by Giambologna. Next comes the Grotto of the Animals, the *selvatico* and the bronze statue of the *Apennine*, also by Ammannati. On the right can be seen the *ortaccio* and the *ragnaia*; to the left and right of the central garden, extensive orchards.

Justus Utens, Villa di Castello, 1599

the citrus trees

Citrus trees – lemons, oranges, citrons, bitter oranges – are distinguished by their upright stance and evergreen leaves. Their cultivation is closely linked to the myths handed down to humanistic culture from the Graeco-Roman world. According to mythology the Hesperides, the nymphs of the West, were the guardians of golden apples that grew in their garden. But the nymphs were unable to prevent Hercules from stealing the apples and taking them to Italy, where they flourished and spread. Citruses are also linked to the myth of eternal Springtime in the Garden of Eden. The plants flower and bear fruit at the same time, thus providing an excellent symbol of the continuity of life.

Between the 16th and 17th centuries citrus trees became common in the villa gardens of Tuscany; having both practical and ornamental functions, they were also used for curative purposes. The cultivation of citruses in Tuscany dates however from more ancient times. Lemon gardens are recorded as existing in Florence already in the Middle Ages, although the trees were at the time planted in the ground and covered with roofing in winter. Cultivation in urns became widespread in the 16th century, along with the custom of building *stanzoni*, or *limonaie*, where the trees were moved to protect them in cold weather. Citrus trees became such a characteristic element of the Tuscan garden that specific gardens or sections of gardens were designated to them. The lemon garden is often located in front of the *limonaia* or near it.

Citruses belong to the family of the *Rutaceae*. The most widely grown types are *Citrus*, to which belong lemons, oranges, citrons and grapefruit; *Fortunella*, to which belongs the kumquat; and *Poncirus*. The latter type has only one species, *Poncirus trifoliata*, a thorny orange used for hedges that are impenetrable to cats.

An extraordinary characteristic of citruses is the development of the varieties and the possibility of creating fruits of strange and monstrous shape, called 'teratological', which were particularly appreciated in the 17th century by the Grand Dukes and the Medici court. Bartolomeo Bimbi depicted them in the late 17th century with 116 varieties and bizarre shapes, in a painting now in the Villa of Poggio a Caiano. One of the most original varieties is the *Citrus aurantium* 'Bizzarria'. It has hybrid fruits, half orange and half citron, colored yellow, orange and green. The 'Bizzarria' was discovered in Florence in 1644 in the garden of the Torre degli Agli.

In the Medicean gardens, Boboli and Castello in particular, enormous collections of citrus trees have been formed. In both gardens there are about one thousand potted citruses, all originating from plants in the ancient collection. This is a collection of priceless value, both botanical and artistic. In the garden of Castello the 'Bizzarria' is lovingly cultivated today by Paolo Galeotti, the gardener who must be hailed for having rediscovered and reproduced through grafting this unique, amazing variety.

Today lemon trees are grown in the Tuscan manner: in the classic 'free' form of a small tree; 'vase-shaped' (held opened by means of props), or 'espaliered'. They have now returned to embellish the finest gardens. Outstanding in this sense is the work of the Tintori family of Pescia. In their splendid nursery they have revived an art that seemed destined to disappear.

The statue of the Apennine

Chronology

1537-1538 Cosimo I commissions Tribolo to design the garden.
1538-1548 Tribolo and Pierino da Vinci work on the fountains of *Fiorenza* and of *Hercules strangling Antaeus.*
1550 After the death of Tribolo, Davide Fortini becomes director of works; he is succeeded by Giorgio Vasari in 1554.
1560-1561 The *selvatico* or wilderness of ilexes and cypresses is planted around the basin with the bronze statue of the *Apennine* sculpted by Ammannati in 1563.
1588-1593 The garden is completed under Grand Duke Ferdinando. In 1599 it is painted by Justus Utens.
Second half of the 18th c. The *limonaia* is built to the west of the villa.
1785-1788 The fountain of *Fiorenza* is moved to the Petraia. Major changes are made in the layout of the garden.

Third decade of the 19th c. Joseph Frietsch, at the service of Ferdinando III di Lorena, transforms most of the vineyards and the *ragnaia* to the east of the villa into an English woods.
After 1918 Villa and garden, formerly Savoia property, pass to the Italian State.
The villa nowadays houses the Accademia della Crusca while the garden is opened to the public.

Villa La Pietra
Restoration with invention

HOW TO ARRIVE

At the locality La Lastra
along the Via Bolognese.
Owner: La Pietra Corporation S.A.
Address: Via Bolognese 120
Bus: 25
tel.: +39 055 5007218
+39 055 5007210
fax: +39 055 5007333
E-mail: villa.lapietra@nyu.edu
Visiting hours: by appointment only

*The garden looking
toward the* tempietto

The great garden extending over a slope facing eastward was laid out starting in 1904 at the desire of the owner, Arthur Acton. The villa had been surrounded by a Baroque garden created by the Capponi family, of which only the lemon garden exists today, which was transformed into an English landscape garden in the 19th century.

In an isolated corner of the garden a stone inscription recalls the leading figures in the great work of transformation: the gardener designers Mariano Ambroziewicz, Pasquale Bonaiuti, Giuseppe Castellucci, Edwin Dodge and H.O. Watson. The list of outstanding figures in the international and local architecture of the times is long. The project, obviously, was grand in scope and did not derive merely from the initiative of an amateur.

The architectural layout reiterates the terraced system typical of the Tuscan garden. Within the system of terraces are then placed *stanze di verzura*, garden rooms inspired by the Baroque gardening tradition. The garden rooms are furnished with architectural elements (largely salvaged from the past) and statues of Venetian provenance (many of them by Bonazza and Orazio Marinali).

Exedras, stone portals, pergolas, vases, balustrades, mascarons of various origin (many of the architectural elements are undoubtedly Tuscan) adorn the rich and varied garden, which remains one of the most striking testimonials to the vogue for antiquarian collections of the times. The preference for classical statues fits well with the strong, precise landscaping concept oriented toward revival of the Italian garden. Harold Acton recalls the creation of the garden in his book *Tuscan Villas*: "The decision to Tuscanize the so-called English garden was taken in 1904", writes Acton. "The garden looking to the south was demolished in the last cen-

tury and restored by my father as he imagined it must have been".

Itinerary of visit

A great cypress avenue bordered in Bengali roses leads to the villa, a building complex of 15th century design transformed several times between the 16th and the 18th centuries. Before the house stood the first great topiaries in yew. Two curious cocks humorously exemplified the style, at once cultured and vernacular, of the early 20th century designers.

Opening out to the left is the *lemon garden* with its magnificent *limonaia*, before which two *osmanto* in enormous vases catch the eye. Elements of great interest are the magnificent **walls decorated** in rustic style, presumably dating from the 18th century. At the center, around a little pool, great clipped hedges of box hold statues and stone benches.

Returning to the entrance to the villa, now the Florence branch of New York University, we enter the garden from the right.

To the side of the building is a fine grotto decorated in a variety of materials. The formal gardens, now undergoing restoration, start in front of the building. Adorned with statues, the gardens offer magnificent views over Florence, looking southward.

Detail of the lemon garden wall

A *pergola* of Banksian roses, splendid in May, crosses the garden up to the great elliptical lawn sprinkled with volunteer thyme plants, at the southern boundary of the property.

To the north a 'garden theatre' with walls of yew trees, recently restored, is decorated with stone statues. The path parallel to theater leads back to a **lawn with a *tempietto***, from where it returns the level of the villa.

The lower garden with the great exedra

To know more

H. Acton, *Tuscan Villas*, London 1973

Web: www.nyu.edu/global/lapietra

Villa Gamberaia
The garden of the Princess

HOW TO ARRIVE

Close to Settignano.
Owner: The Zalum family
Address: Via del Rossellino 72,
Settignano
Bus: 10
tel.: +39 055 697205 / 697090
E-mail: info@villagamberaia.com
Visiting hours:
9:00 am - 6:00 pm
Admission: 10,00 €, reduced 8,00 €
for students. Visits by previous
phone call or e-mail, expecially
for groups.
Accessible to the disabled
Restrooms
Bookshop

The entrance avenue

Villa Gamberaia is one of the truly magic places in the world. The splendid landscape, the views of city and countryside, the architecture of the villa and the garden are justly famous, making it one of the most renowned gardens.

Not much is known of the first 15th century building, consisting in all probability of the small construction beside which the *limonaia* was built later. The history of the garden starts around 1610, when Zanobi di Andrea Lapi had the villa built. The garden, which certainly already existed, was enlarged in the 18th century when the property passed to the Capponi family, who owned it until 1854.

During the second half of the 19th century the villa changed ownership several times until 1896, when it was bought by Princess Ghyka. It became the Princess' favorite residence, and she built a **water *parterre*** as replacement for the 18th century *parterre de broderie*. This part of the garden has been completely transformed. An 18th century *cabreo* shows the Baroque design of an elegant *parterre* that ended in a *garenna,* or rabbit island. The elliptical shape of the *garenna* was reiterated in the belvedere of cypresses and the semicircular pool. The four sections of the parterre were repeated, but with the full and empty areas inverted and flowerbeds turned into pools of water.

Borders of lavender, iris, lilies, tree roses and olean-
ders were reflected in pools lined by hedges of box.
Images of the garden in flower, soon after its completion, have come down to us from numerous photog-
raphers of the early 20th century.

The central element of the garden is a great grassy
avenue, the bowling green. It forms a longitudinal axis
of 225 meters that opens to the south onto the Arno
Valley and ends to the north in a nymphaeum built
into the hillside, surrounded by ancient cypresses. The
transverse axis, about half as long, crosses the villa
and forms the other main element of composition, the
gabinetto rustico, with elliptical plan and walls decorated with shells and various materials. Through four
asymmetrical stairways the gabinetto leads, on one
side, to the first selvatico to the south, on the other to
the lemon garden and the second selvatico to the north.

Itinerary of visit

From the exedra that forms the entrance on Via del
Rossellino a gate opens onto the **cypress avenue**. The
trees line both sides of the path like thick curtains. A
visual corridor leads to the villa, which shows its northern side to the visitor. The main facade looks to the
east, in the direction of Florence. The visitor's gaze is
guided along the gently sloping avenue up to the
house. Here there are no distracting elements and
no visual opening onto the surrounding landscape or
the garden. Arriving at the house we find, on the left,
two arches that link the first floor to the chapel; on the
right is a lawn. A great pine tree dominates and bounds
the view over the valley. Passing under the side arcades
of the villa we find the **bowling green**, the axis that
ideally and physically links the Arno River to the hill.
This is not a rigidly symmetrical axis. One of the most

The modern parterre

Above:
the bowling-green

Bottom:
the modern
parterre in a photo
from the early
20th century

the modern
parterre as it
appears today

On the right and left sides, two double ramps of stairs lead to one of the *selvatici* and to the lemon garden. The building on the right, its interior structured like a harmonious 15th century house, is in all probability the first core of the property owned by the Gamberelli family in the locality already called *Gamberaia* in the 15th century (from the name of the pond for *gamberi*, or crayfish). In winter the great *limonaia* shelters the important collection of citrus trees, which are moved

distinctive features of the garden design is in fact its flexible architectural scheme, adapted with sensitivity to the logic of the place. From here we follow a grassy path to enter the **gabinetto di roccaglia**, a striking architectural element that links the villa level with that of the *limonaia* and the two *selvatici*. In the shape of an elongated ellipse, it has walls richly decorated with niches and *terra-cotta* statues. From the back wall emerge some figures, today partially destroyed. The *giochi d'acqua*, still existing, are controlled from a room under a stairway. Head-high jets of water were designed to drench visitors as they paused to admire the splendid, harmonious sandstone fountain.

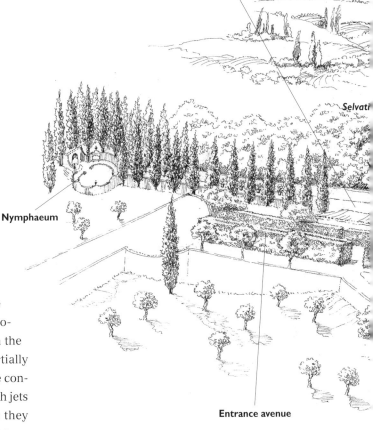

Bowling-green

Selvati

Nymphaeum

Entrance avenue

in spring to the ends of the four lawns. The **limonaia garden**, divided into four lawns, is embellished by a mixed border of perennials where arboreal peonies and Albertine **roses flower** in splendor. The *selvatico* of ancient ilexes, the ground below them carpeted with periwinkles, is linked again to the bowling green. From the thick shade of the *selvatico* visitors thus pass, in an alternation filled with symbolic meaning, to the bright sunlight on the lawn.

The gabinetto di roccaglia

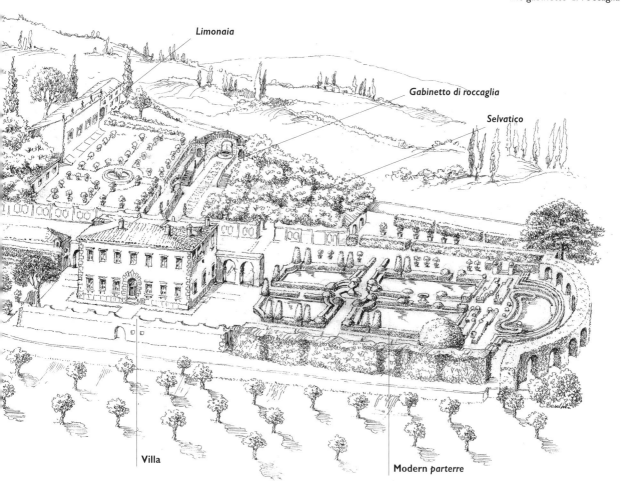

Limonaia

Gabinetto di roccaglia

Selvatico

Villa

Modern *parterre*

From the lemon garden a path leads on to the *selvatico* to the south, where the *gabinetto di roccaglia*, the stone fountain and the fine pavement of colored pebbles can be seen from above. Through the *selvatico* we go to the water *parterre*, pausing below the majestic Corsican pine tree to enjoy a magnificent view over the Arno Valley.

We then go on to the water *parterre* created by Princess Ghyka.

The arcade geometry of the **cypress belvedere**, where climbing roses are entwined high in the cypress branches, continues in the pattern of the hedges and the spherical shapes of the box bushes, while yew trees impose a vertical rhythm on the space enclosed by the *parterre*.

From here we can go on to the great lawn before the villa where a glimpse of Florence appears beyond the olive groves. Going around the building we return to the bowling green and continue in the direction of the nymphaeum.

On the left the long construction houses the chapel and the ancient room where the game of *pallacorda* was played.

The nymphaeum, surrounded by cypresses, is preceded by a circular lawn surrounded by a wall, enclosing an area that is both majestic and intimate. It is a theater, probably designed for music and rendered enigmatic by the god emerging from the niche carved out of the hill (it may be Dionysus, as suggested by the shepherds and musicians appearing beside him).

The tree roses in flower

In April visitors can admire the splendid collection of azaleas blossoming along the leading to the villa.

To know more

M. Pozzana, *Una guida per conoscere Villa Gamberaia*, Florence 1998.

Web: www.villagamberaia.com

The exedra belvedere

Pelargoniums in terra-cotta urn

Chronology

1412 Documents record property owned by the Gamberelli family in the locality known as *Gamberaia*.

1610 Zanobi di Andrea Lapi purchases land at *Gamberaia*.

1717 After the death of Giovanni di Andrea Lapi the villa becomes the property of Vincenzio Maria and Piero Capponi. The Capponi family embellish the garden with new elements.

1854 Vincenzio Capponi sells La Gamberaia to Pietro Favreau. From this date up to the end of the century the property is sold several times.

1896 Catherine Jeanne Keshko, the Rumanian wife of Prince Eugenio Ghyka, buys the villa.

1910 Pietro Porcinai, the great Florentine landscape artist, is born in the vicinity of the villa. Martino, Pietro's father, works for Princess Ghyka as head gardener. With Luigi Messeri he creates the modern garden of Villa Gamberaia, so famous that it soon becomes a model for numerous other gardens (for example, that of the castle of Ambleville in the Val d'Oise).

1924 The Baroness von Ketteler purchases the villa.

1944 A German command in retreat sets fire to the building, used as cartographic center of the German Army. Garden and villa are severely damaged.

1952 The villa is donated to the Holy See.

1954 Marcello Marchi buys the villa and carries out major restoration work. Since 1955 the garden, restored, is open to visitors.

1988 The villa is inhabited by Nerina Von Erdber Krscenziewski, the Lithuanian wife of Marcello Marchi, until her death in 1990.

1995 The property is assigned to Luigi Zalum and his wife Franca Marchi.

Villa La Quiete
The refuge of the Palatine Electress

HOW TO ARRIVE

Between Serpiolle and Careggi.
Address:
Via della Quiete 14
Buses: 14, 20
tel.: +39 055 452304
At present closed for restoration
and transfer of ownership

The complex is composed of the villa and a church built between 1686 and 1689 by Pier Francesco Silvani. The religious vocation of the site originated with the foundation of the Congregazione delle Minime Ancelle della SS. Trinità, which established here the Conservatorio delle Signore Montalve. It was then Anna Maria Luisa, the Palatine Electress and last member of the Medici family, who definitively transformed the place of her own spiritual refuge, inextricably mingling sacred and profane elements. Between 1724 and 1727 the villa-convent was thus adorned with a splendid garden designed by Pietro Giovannozzi in collaboration with Sebastiano Rapi, the Boboli gardener. Testifying to the deeply religious nature of Anna Maria Luisa is the fountain that decorates the outer walls, with the group of *Jesus Christ and the Samaritan Woman*.

Itinerary of visit
Although small in size the garden is extraordinarily interesting, conserving one of the very rare surviving

ragnaie, woods for hunting considered a fundamental element in the creation of a garden for the nobility since the 15th century. The *ragnaia* of Villa La Quiete runs all along the eastern side of the garden and is formed of long parallelepipeds planted to ilex and bordered by high hedges of laurel and laurustine. Along these parallelepipeds, nets were once stretched to capture birds. Within the *ragnaia* the *camere di*

The group of Jesus Christ and the Samaritan Woman

View of the city

A tree-lined corridor in the ragnaia

verzura, or garden rooms, with benches in stone or *terra-cotta,* are still well preserved. In summer this was a cool place in which to rest and listen to the birds singing. Here we can easily see how *ragnaie,* although designed for bird-catching, were also places of delightful repose.

Below the terrace on which the villa faces is the lower garden, with an orchard bordered in box, vases and potted citrus trees. On the left, through the encircling wall, we enter the *limonaia.* On the northern side an informal *boschetto* has been added.

The villa

Le Balze
A garden-terrace

The theme, not an easy one, has been brilliantly developed in the overall composition, centered around the villa which opens at the sides onto the gardens laid out in a series of *stanze di verzura*, or **garden rooms**. On the south side a **terrace** that is splendidly panoramic although small in size overlooks the city. In the back, towards the hillside, steps out leading to the upper terrace have been carved. A *pergola* ends in a broad sheltering roof.

The most original feature of the garden is the grotto that opens

HOW TO ARRIVE

In the immediate vicinity of Fiesole.
Owner: Georgetown University
Address: Via Vecchia Fiesolana 26, Fiesole
Bus: 7
tel.: +39 055 59208
E-mail: info@villalebalze.org
Visiting hours: Mon.-Fri.
8:30 am - 3:30 pm
Closed August and holidays
Visits only by previous phone call or e-mail
Free donation
Partially accessible to the disabled

The narrow terrace in front of the villa

One of the garden rooms

This garden is one of the finest achievements of Cecil Pinsent (1884-1963), the refined English landscape artist who worked in Florence from the 1910s up to World War II. The breathtaking panorama and the ingenuity with which Pinsent exploited the possibilities of the site make this one of the most interesting initiatives in the trend toward revival of the formal garden.

Situated at the same height as Villa Medici on the southern slope of the Fiesole hill, the villa (now the headquarters of Georgetown University) and garden were constructed starting in 1914 by Pinsent and the historian of architecture Geoffrey Scott. The client, the American philosopher Charles Augustus Strong, commissioned Pinsent and Scott to direct the construction of the building and garden on a long, narrow terrace.

The lemon garden

below the ramp of stairs, in the finest tradition of the Italian Baroque garden.

The garden is entered from Via Vecchia Fiesolana. A *boschetto* of yew trees trimmed to shape forms a first garden room. Several of these 'rooms' are crossed to enter the **lemon garden**, divided into four sections and ornamented by a central pond. Two openings in the western wall lead to the terrace overlooking Florence, behind the house. Continuing beyond the house we find a last garden room before a *boschetto* of ilexes dis-

tinguished by an unusual *romitorio*, or hermit's retreat. At the end of the garden, which drifts off into the countryside with borders of lavender and iris, stands the stone statue of a hermit.

To know more
M. Fantoni, H. Flores, J. Pfordresher, *Cecil Pinsent and his Gardens in Tuscany*, Florence 1995.

Web: www11.georgetown.edu/oip/os/villalebalze

Villa I Tatti
A revival of the Italian garden

HOW TO ARRIVE

Between Maiano, in the vicinity
of Fiesole, and Settignano.
Owners: The President and fellows
of Harvard College
Address: Via di Vincigliata 26, Fiesole
Bus: 10
tel.: +39 055 603251
E-mail: info@itatti.it
Visiting hours: by reservation, only
on Tuesday and Wednesday
at 3:00 pm and 4:00 pm
(maximum 8 persons)
Free admission
Difficult access to the disabled
Guided visits
Restrooms

based on the great formal suggestions of topiary art.
I Tatti is one of the first gardens designed in the Italian style with the clear intention of revival, in the de-

The lower grotto

sire to re-establish the formal harmony attained by the gardens of the past, such as Villa Gamberaia. Pinsent declared his admiration for the art of the Italian garden, insisting that it was possible to learn to design a garden by taking as model those of the past.

Villa I Tatti is the manifest expression of this concept, shared by many intellectuals in the highly cultured and sophisticated British colony residing in the villas scattered over the hills around Florence at the turn of the century.

Itinerary of visit

On leaving the fine **formal garden** that stands before the villa and passing through the *limonaia*, the great ***parterre***, so beautiful as to seem ancient, appears in all its splendor. Four terraced tiers slope gently downward, concluding in the last section where the

Laid out on the gentle slope of the Vincigliata hill, between Poggio Gherardo and Poggio al Vento, the garden was conceived as an outdoor extension of the house, a great *camera di verzura* to be discovered with delight upon entering the *limonaia*.

Cecil Pinsent, the English architect and landscape designer, had only recently come to Italy when Bernard Berenson, the renowned art historian and cosmopolitan, and his wife Mary commissioned him to direct the work of creating a garden on the property they were then restoring. The historian of architecture Geoffrey Scott was also involved in this initiative.

The work, begun in 1911, concluded a few years later with the extraordinary reinvention of a Baroque garden skillfully structured as concerns spatial effects and central path, decorated with fine gravel patterns in homage to 17th century tradition, drifts off into a meadow.

Hedges of box design complex geometric motifs and a series of spires confers a marked rhythm on the high evergreen hedges. No concession to color can be seen in a garden that deliberately emphasizes the plastic

The avenue of cypresses

and decorative aspects of plants clipped in topiary form.

At the bottom of the terrace a double flight of stairs leads to the *selvatico* of ilexes planted geometrically according to the finest Renaissance tradition. Parallel to the garden, on the eastern side, a broad avenue leads to a rustic **grotto**.

To know more

M. Fantoni, H. Flores, J. Pfordresher, *Cecil Pinsent and his Gardens in Tuscany*, Florence 1995.

Web: www.itatti.it

The garden seen from below

Fonte Lucente
A garden lover's dream

The garden near the villa

HOW TO ARRIVE

On the road that leads
from Fiesole to Montebeni.
Owner: Fondazione Parchi
Monumentali Bardini e Peyron
Address: Via di Vincigliata 2, Fiesole
Bus: 7
For reservations:
tel.: +39 055 20066206
E-mail: mg.geri@bardinipeyron.it
Visiting hours: by reservation, only
Monday and Wednesday 10:00 am-
4:00 pm, closed for holidays
During some periods in spring
and summer, open every day
without need for reservations
Groups min 5 persons
Admission: 10,00 €
Guided visits upon request in sev-
eral languages
Restrooms
Partial access to the disabled

Situated on the slopes of the Fiesole hillside, the garden of Fonte Lucente is the creation of Paolo Peyron, who was its owner. Throughout his life he designed, transformed, organized and adorned it with passionate enthusiasm and rare sensitivity.

Angelo Peyron purchased the villa in 1914 and commissioned the architect Ugo Giovannozzi (1876-1957) to transform the building in keeping with the eclectic style then in vogue. Paolo Peyron inherited the property in 1919 and took residence there in 1934, beginning the work of creating a garden that has been developed since then, organically and consistently, almost without interruption.

Damage undergone in World War II called for reconstruction and work was intensified, giving rise to the **Italian garden**, the terraces, the stairways, and the space for music dedicated to Riccardo Muti with a belvedere on the lake, beds of box, a pond, the woods adorned with antique garden architecture and numerous **statues** coming from the Veneto (about eighty in number, distributed throughout the garden and the woods).

At Fonte Lucente water is a fundamental element. There are 29 fountains built of elements of various provenance.

The **terraces** of the garden slope down along an ideal longitudinal axis, closed off by backdrops of tall cypresses in such a way as to offer a view of the city, which is seen as if through a telescopic lens (Paolo Peyron said that he created a stage with the city as backdrop). On the eastern side of the property a **pond** has been built, on which faces the area dedicated to music.

A visit to the villa in spring is recommended, to see the flowering of the wisteria, when the wall of the terrace in the first garden glows with a splendid indigo color.

To know more
I. Romitti, *Il bosco di Fonte Lucente,* Florence 1997.
Web: www.bardinipeyron.it

The lower parterre

The pond

Above:
a statue
in the woods

Bottom:
the central path

the garden seen
from below;
in the background,
the villa

"Many times I have been asked
what is the secret
of the beauty of my
garden. I have answered that
this garden reflects my life,
with its joys, its grief, its loves
and disappointments.
The intense atmosphere
breathed in the garden
derives from the fact
that all of my feelings, thoughts
and doubts have remained
here. Perhaps it has been
the place of a particular
concentration of interests,
an environment that reflects
my life".

Paolo Peyron

The garden in front of the chapel

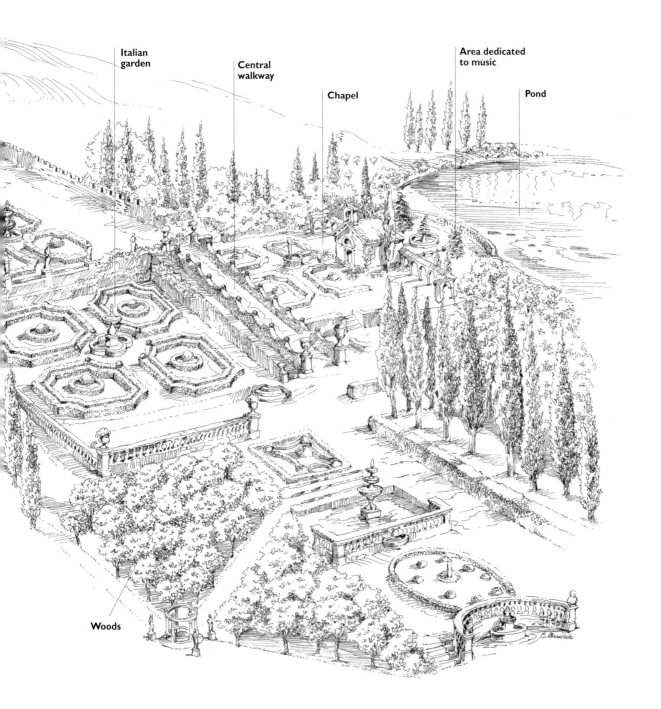

Italian garden

Central walkway

Chapel

Area dedicated to music

Pond

Woods

Villa Medici
The invention of a landscape

HOW TO ARRIVE

In the immediate vicinity of Fiesole.
Privately owned.
Address: Via Fra' Giovanni Angelico
2, Fiesole
Bus: 7
fax: +39 055 2398994
Visiting hours: Mon.-Fri. 9:00 am-
1:00 pm by appointment only
(for groups and upon presentation
of request in writing)
Admission: 6,00 €

B uilt on the side of the Fiesole hill turned toward Florence, at a point where the slope becomes steeper, Villa Medici dominates the landscape, the house admirably harmonizing with the surrounding terraces of its garden.

We owe this construction, certainly the most panoramic of the Medicean properties from the 15th century, to Giovanni di Cosimo de' Medici, fascinated by the stupendous view and by the modernity of this relationship with the landscape.

Giovanni, a highly cultured art lover and expert director of the Medicean bank, commissioned Michelozzo di Bartolomeo to build the villa. The garden was designed according to an innovative plan: a series of terraces reiterates the farming technique of cultivating terraced land, but transforms it into something noble and monumental. The villa co-exists with the garden that surrounds its two wings; one to the east, opening onto the terraced entrance level; the other to the west, looking over a garden of smaller size. We know that already in the 15th century citrus trees were cultivated here: bitter oranges grown on espaliers, for example, protected in winter by seasonal roofing, along with *incarnate* roses (*Rosa x alba incarnata*).

The garden is divided into two main terraced levels. A long avenue leads through the ilex woods to the first terrace on a level with the ground floor of the villa. To the left of the entrance is the late 18th century belvedere that dramatically frames an extraordinary view of the city.

The lower terrace

To the left can be seen the elegant *limonaia* dating from the same period. The citrus urns are arranged around sectors of lawn bounded by stone curbs, dominated by two great paulownias (*Paulownia tomentosa*). To the right, on a slightly higher level, are climbing roses grown by the pegging down technique, in vogue during the second half of the 19th century (the rose shoots are fixed to pegs or chains).

Leaning against the right wall is a splendid *espalier* of bitter oranges, recalling the important collections of citrus trees that was the pride of the garden in the

15th century. We know in fact that in 1455
melaranci, (*melangoli* or bitter oranges,
Citrus Aurantium and *limoncelli, Citrus
limon* 'Neapolitanum') were grown here.
The long pergola flaming with Banksian
roses, created in the early 20th century by
Cecil Pinsent, leads to the **lower terrace**,
divided into four beds: two consisting of
lawns shaded by magnolia trees, the other two with box bushes.

To the west of the villa is a little garden
with box hedges, magnolias and a fine
central fountain.

To know more

Giardini medicei, edited by C. Acidini,
Milan 1996.

I. Romitti, M. Zoppi, *Guida ai giardini
di Fiesole,* Florence 2000.

D. Mazzini, S. Martini, *Villa Medici
a Fiesole: Leon Battista Alberti e il prototipo
di villa rinascimentale,* Florence 2004.

Web: www.villamedicifiesole.it

The garden in front of the villa

Chronology

1451-1457 Michelozzo di Bartolomeo, commissioned by Giovanni de' Medici, builds the villa.
1469 Lorenzo the Magnificent inherits the villa. Poliziano is a frequent guest and recalls the beauty of the place in his poetry, contributing to its mythical fame.
1492 An inventory compiled at the death of Lorenzo describes the garden:''...a garden behind said palace with several small orchards and fields walled and enclosed in masonry and a piece of land known as garden with cypresses and other trees forming a *boschetto* and a plot of vegetable garden''.
1671 The villa is sold by Cosimo III to Vincenzo di Cosimo del Sera.
1772 Lady Orford becomes owner of the property. She

commissions Niccolò Gaspero Paoletti to transform the villa. Paoletti creates a new carriage entrance, new grotesque-style decorations and a pavilion facing the villa. The work is completed in 1779.
1862 The new owner William Blundell Spence widens the entrance avenue and finds a section of Etruscan wall (as can be read in a stone inscription at the entrance).
1911 Lady Sybil Cutting, a friend of Bernard Berenson, asks Geoffrey Scott (who will become her husband) and Cecil Pinsent to direct the work of renovation. Pinsent creates a neo-15th century garden on the lower terrace, adding a long rose *pergola,* and transforms the garden on the west side by planting four magnolias.
1959 The villa is purchased by the Marchi Mazzini family.

Villa Corsi Salviati
A garden of statues and flowers

HOW TO ARRIVE

In the center of Sesto Fiorentino.
Owner: the Guicciardini Corsi
Salviati family
Address: Via Gramsci 462, Sesto
Fiorentino
fax: +39 055 2346863
Visiting hours: by appointment
only (upon presentation of re-
quest in writing)

*At right:
detail of the
encircling wall*

*Next page:
two views of the
Baroque* parterre

Villa Corsi Salviati, today the Florence headquarters of the University of Michigan, offers a very clear example of the changes made in a Tuscan garden over the course of its long history. A fine garden of statues, it has basins of water, fountains and beautifully decorated walls. Situated on the plain, it offers no memorable views of countryside or city, but is nonetheless splendid for the balanced linking of its spaces and carefully planned details.

The simple 16th century garden (appearing in a painting on the ground floor of the house) was enlarged in the 17th century with the addition of pools, statues, an orchard and a *selvatico*. In the 18th century the great *ragnaia*, over two hundred meters long, was planted and the vast Baroque-style *parterre* of flowers was constructed. Then at the beginning of 20th century the garden was restored again. At the turn of the 19th century English visitors were already struck by the beauty of a garden that, although dating from the Baroque period, was deemed to be of maximum interest. Great was their surprise on discovering, beyond the **encircling wall**, a park abounding in statues, pools and walls decorated with *pietra spugna* and marble tesserae. The garden is composed of several different zones linked to one another. The visitor passes through a succession of 'rooms' with a growing sense of wonder. First comes the ornamental *parterre* with its precious flowerbeds bounded by hedges of dwarf box; then the lemon garden, today a simple lawn, in front of the *limonaia*; and lastly the English woods. Within the woods the fine *teatro di verzura*, or garden theater, and a maze of box were created.

Itinerary of visit

A secondary entrance on via Gramsci leads to the garden theater with its backdrop of cypress trees dominated by the statue of *Apollo*. Around the theater grow centuries-old ilexes, which may have belonged to the villa's first *selvatico*. Half hidden by the trees is a little artificial lake with a cast iron bridge and a small **maze** of boxwood modeled after the one at Hampton Court.

At the center of the garden is a ***parterre*** of flowers with a complex geometric design. From a rectangular

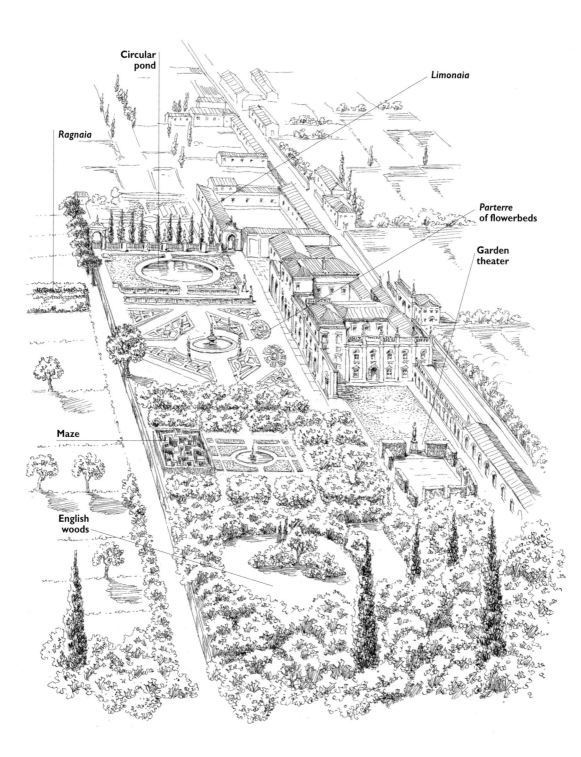

Circular pond

Limonaia

Ragnaia

Parterre of flowerbeds

Garden theater

Maze

English woods

The circular basin

with a fine wrought iron gate and statues on pilasters separates the *parterre* from the *limonaia* and its lawn. The *limonaia* has now become a theater.

The facade of the villa extends to the west with two singular aviaries. The one on the right is today an open loggia with beautiful frescoed decorations.

basin adorned by statues of the four seasons at the corners leads a waterway that flows through the *ragnaia*. Beyond the **circular basin** with nymphs a wall

To know more

G. Guicciardini Corsi Salviati, *La villa Corsi a Sesto*, Florence 1937.

Chronology

1502 Simone di Jacopo Corsi buys the property from Luca di Andrea Carnesecchi.
1593-1603 Jacopo, Giulio and Bardo Corsi enlarge the building.
1632 Giovanni and Lorenzo di Jacopo Corsi undertake a second stage of work. Gherardo Silvani is probably responsible for the architectural part, while Baccio del Bianco, between 1640 and 1641, decorates some rooms with paintings that are now lost.
1644 A map documents the work on the garden, which appears divided into sectors separated by walls: the flower garden, the *selvatico*, the orchard, a fish-pond with exedra and a rabbit lawn.
1729 Antonio Corsi enlarges the villa and transforms the garden. The rectangular pool and the canal with 13 little waterfalls are built.
1815 Amerigo Corsi begins transforming the eastern part of the garden into an English woods.
1866 Exotic plants are introduced.
1907 Giulio Giucciardini Corsi Salviati begins to restore the property.

A photograph from the second half of the 19th century which documents the changes in the garden

Pratolino
The Villa Demidoff Park

HOW TO ARRIVE

In the immediate
vicinity of Pratolino.
Address: Via Fiorentina 276,
Pratolino, Vaglia
Bus: 25A
tel.: +39 055 409427
+39 055 409558 / +39 055 408071
fax: +39 055 409272
E-mail: parcpra@provincia.fi.it
Visiting hours:
Apr.-Oct.:
Sat.-Sun. 10:00 am - 7:00 pm
Free admission
Always open for groups making
reservations by phone call
Accessible to the disabled
Restrooms
Café-restaurant
Bookshop

created on the basis of alchemistic concepts. The basement of the Medicean villa held an amazing series of grottoes where visitors were struck by *giochi d'acqua*, automata and music. A great number of sculptures and architectural structures marked the stages of a

The avenue leading from the entrance

journey through the 'park of the ancients' to the 'park of the moderns', located to the south, along a longitudinal axis that led from the avenue of spouting jets to the villa and then to the statue of the *Apennine*, the maze and the fountain of *Jove*.

The 16th century geometric structure was totally demolished by Ferdinando III di Lorena, who called upon Joseph Frietsch to redesign the park around 1818. The landscape artist produced a masterpiece at the price of drastic changes, creating a romantic park where a 16th century garden once lay. The broad, luminous landscape designed by Frietsch is unique in Tuscany, and great meadows, skillfully modeled, alternate today with thick woods of ancient oak trees.

Itinerary of visit

From the entrance on Via Bolognese an avenue lined with horse chestnuts leads to the buildings of the new

Pratolino is today the most important landscape park in Tuscany. Its complex history spans immense changes in taste, fashions and trends in garden art. It is undoubtedly the most important example of transition from the late Renaissance garden to the modern English-style one. Its 19th century transformation resulted in virtually total destruction of the Late Renaissance park of Francesco I de' Medici, the model in its day for the most important European parks.

The Medicean park was famous for its grottoes, *giochi d'acqua* (waterworks) and the automata with their enigmatic meanings standing along the paths, probably

the Apennine
by Giambologna

The colossal statue-fountain, standing at the center of park, is its fulcrum and symbol. Created around 1580 by Giambologna, it represents an old man seated, leaning over the basin of water below in which his image is reflected. Numerous jets of water, coming also from the head, transform the statue into a fountain. A submissive giant, man/mountain, man/river, the *Apennine* in its symbolic complexity suggests a myriad of interpretations. Originally, the giant contained several grottoes within it. Of these only one, carved out of the back of the colossus, still conserves part of the decorations in *pietra spugna* and calcareous concretions dating from the late 17th century restoration. The grotto below appears instead as a simple rustic grotto despoiled of all of its original decoration, but no less hauntingly evocative. The *Apennine* was constructed by the technique of sculpture in masonry, with an iron framework and gravel underlayer covered in brick and plaster. At the foot of the statue is a semicircular basin. In the time of Ferdinando III it was transformed into a very natural looking pool.

Above:
Villa Demidoff

Bottom:
the statue
of the Mugnone

spugna, now divided into two parts; the maze of laurel bushes was filled with *spugna*.

The fountain marked the northernmost part of the 16th century park, where a wall closed off the property. Now instead we can continue up to the Montili belvedere, with its splendid view over the valley toward Florence. Returning to the *Apennine*, in crossing the great meadow we reach the place where Buontalenti's villa once stood.

To the right a stone stairway leads up to a hexagonal-shaped chapel surrounded by a loggia, designed by

farmhouse and stables. The main body, built by Buontalenti, was altered in the first half of the 19th century by the addition of the shorter wing of the building. From here we go on to the little lake before the statue of the **Apennine**, the world-famous sculpture by Giambologna with its *giochi d'acqua*. In summer the lake is covered with a lovely patchwork of water iris, lotus and water lilies. Behind the *Apennine*, through winding paths opening onto carefully modeled meadows, we go on to what was at the time of Francesco I the 'park of the ancients', arriving at the fountain of *Jove* to find what remains of the great

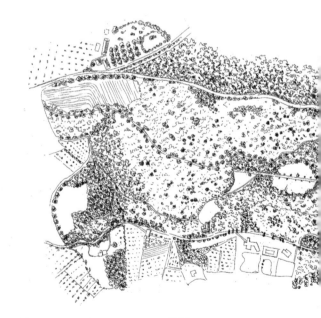

I Entrance	8 Villa
2 Old post stage	9 Great aviary
3 Villetta	10 Statue of the *Mugnone*
4 Buontalenti's chapel	11 Grotto of Cupid
5 Stables	12 Avenue of spouting jets
6 Statue of the *Apennine*	13 *Gamberaie*
7 Fountain of *Jove*	14 Montili Belvedere

Buontalenti and transformed during the course of the 19th century. Nearby is the tomb of Maria Demidoff.

Nothing remains today of the 16th century villa but the entrance, formed of two symmetrical ramps of stairs framing the fountain of the *Mugnone*.

At the sides, under the stairs, were once placed the first two grottoes: the grotto of *Fame* and that of *Pan with the nymph Syringa*. The grottoes were famous for the automata moved by water-powered mechanisms.

Of these hydraulic and mechanical marvels there exist today only the **statue of the *Mugnone*** by Giambologna and the remains of the decoration at the entrance, rediscovered by Princess Demidoff a few years before World War II.

In front of the villa, and on the same axis, begins the monumental avenue that ends in the 'avenue of jets', another marvel of the park. Before descending to the southern part we can turn to the right to visit the villetta. In front of the villetta is the grotto of *Cupid,* which once held a statue of the demigod.

Other entrance

the vegetation

In the 16th century the park covered nearly 20 hectares. It was surrounded by fields and farms worked by tenant farmers. Silver fir trees, once the distinctive feature of the park, formed an extensive woods in the northern part, around the statue of the *Apennine* and beyond. To the east the park was bounded by *ragnaie* composed mainly of ilexes. The maze was built of laurel. Between the 18th and 19th centuries the vegetation of the park (enlarged to 160 hectares by the encapsulation of farmlands) underwent great change, finally assuming its present aspect, dominated by oaks introduced on a large scale. Among the varieties of oak the most majestic trees are the cerris, the English oak and the pubescent oak (all belonging to the genus *Quercus*).

Great trees in the park

Returning along the axis of the villa we find what was once Buontalenti's great aviary. At left are five pools of fresh water used for raising crayfish, the *gamberaie*, extensively altered in the early 19th century. Before the *gamberaie* stood the fountain of the *Springs*, a complex work designed by Ammannati. Today only a few elements survive, at the Bargello Museum.

Through the avenue of jets we reach the bottom of the park, beyond the 16th century boundary. The fountain of the *Washwoman* once stood in the 'park of the moderns'. Joseph Frietsch added a new landscape park beyond the fountain. In doing so he exploited the steep slope of the area and used what remained at the time of the agricultural structures once belonging to the Medicean farm surrounding the park, the flour mill and the olive mill in particular.

Water became once more the crucial element, with the landscape artist laying out rock gardens, waterfalls and *orridi* of great beauty (now not included in the visitors' itinerary).

To know more

Pratolino. Villa Demidoff. Storia, Arte, Natura, edited by Zeffiro Ciuffoletti, Florence 1990.

Web: www.provincia.fi.it/pratolino

the Medicean aqueduct

Below the park of Francesco I a thick network of galleries and chambers for various mechanisms and for decanting water formed the arteries and veins of the garden, representing the peak of technical/hydraulic knowledge of the times. The whole array of marvels (fountains, grottoes with waterworks and *automata*) struck visitors to Pratolino with wonder, amazed at the ingenious blend of art and technology.

Justus Utens,
Parco di Pratolino
(1599)

Chronology

1568 Francesco I de' Medici, the alchemist prince, purchases land at Pratolino.

1570-1575 Bernardo Buontalenti, the favorite architect of Francesco I, designs the villa and starts building it.

1579-1580 The park and farm are created. The *Apennine* and numerous other grottoes and fountains are completed.

1587 Francesco I dies. Don Antonio, his natural son, inherits the property, but it is Ferdinando I, Francesco's brother, who continues the work.

Before 1710 The great maze in the northern part of the park and the artificial mountain erected behind the *Apennine* are demolished. In their place G.B. Foggini creates the stone dragon.

1737 Pratolino slowly falls into ruin, in a degradation that continues up to 1814.

1773 Some statues are brought to Boboli. The furnishings of the villa are despoiled.

1814 Ferdinando III di Lorena returns to Tuscany and commissions the landscape artist Joseph Frietsch to transform the park into a modern English landscape garden.

1821 The villa, in a poor state of conservation, is demolished.

1820 The architect Luigi de Cambray Digny creates the Montili belvedere, an elegant neo-classical *pavilion*.

1845 The park becomes the personal property of the Grand Duke, remaining so even after the Lorraines abandon Tuscany.

1872 Pratolino is sold to Prince Paolo Demidoff.

1969 After the death of the last Princess Maria Demidoff, the estate is sold at auction.

1981 The Province of Florence buys the park of Pratolino and opens it to the public.

Villa di Bellosguardo
The garden of the opera singer Caruso

Situated southeast of Ponte a Signa, the villa lies at the center of a park atop the hill known as Colle Alberti. Seen from above, the estate is the dominating feature of the surrounding landscape, its lozenge shape standing out clearly from the geometric pattern of the fields around it. Behind two gates opening onto the road, the main one to the north, the service entrance to the south, appears the splendid wooded backdrop of the *selvatico*.

The layout of the garden dates from the last twenty years of the 17th century and was probably designed by Giuliano Ciaccheri for Orazio Ruberto Pucci. Today the villa consists of two symmetrical bodies joined by a *portico*, built around 1915 by the architect Sabatini for one of the villa's last owners, the tenor Enrico Caruso. Enclosed between the two buildings and the *portico* are geometric *parterres* of box, with the collection of potted citrus trees.

HOW TO ARRIVE

West of Florence.
Address: Via di Bellosguardo 54, Lastra a Signa
Bus: 72, SITA from Piazza Adua
tel.: +39 055 8721783
E-mail: info@villacaruso.it
Visiting hours:
Mar.: Sat. 2:30-6:00 pm; Sun. 9:30 am-12:30 pm, 2:30-6:00 pm.
Apr.: Sat. 3:00-7:00 pm; Sun. 9:30 am-12:30 pm, 3:00-7:00 pm;
May: Sat. 3:00-7:30 pm; Sun. 9:30 am-12:30 pm, 3:00-7:30 pm.
June: Sat. 3:30-7:30 pm; Sun. 9:30 am-12:00 pm, 3:30-7:30 pm.
Jul.-Aug.: Sat. 4:00-8:00 pm; Sun. 9:30 am-12:00 pm, 3:00-7:30 pm.
Sept.: Sat. 3:30-7:30 pm; Sun. 9:00 am-12:00 pm, 3:00-7:30 pm;
Oct.: Sat. 3:00-6:30 pm; Sun. 9:00 am-12:00 pm, 3:00-6:30 pm.
Nov.: Sat. 2:00-5:00 pm; Sun. 9:00 am-12:00 pm, 2:00-5:00 pm.
Dec.: Sat. 2:00-5:00 pm; Sun. 9:00 am-12:00 pm, 2:00-5:00 pm
Free admission
Accessible to the disabled
Restrooms

A corner of the park with the column erected upon completion of the work ordered by Enrico Caruso

The garden is distinguished by a rhomboid design that fits majestically into the landscape. A system of perspective views harmoniously links the park to its surrounding countryside (a clear perception of the original design is now unfortunately hindered by the fencing added by Caruso).

The garden is entered through the southern gate, the second one for visitors coming from Ponte a Signa. Passing beside the custodian's house, built by Caruso, we arrive at a broader tree-lined space inviting the visitor to pause to admire the scenery.

O ver the curves of the winding country road that leads from Ponte a Signa to Malmantile, through cultivated fields, olive groves and woods, we arrive at the Villa di Bellosguardo.

The formal garden

The central path, the only one that slopes gently up-hill, leads to the forecourt of the villa between thick curtains of ilex, laurel and viburnum.

The two main bodies of the building are famed by wide lawns, bordered in box. The one on the right was originally the old *casino di delizia*, probably built in the late 16th century by Abbey Alessandro Pucci (thought to be designed by Giovanni Antonio Dosio). On the side of the building, near a well, a stone inscription in Latin along with its translation exhorts the guest to indulge in meditation.

The second building, originally small in size and destined to be used for storing grain, was enlarged over the years, reaching its present size at the time of Caruso. Through the portal that opens in the wall between the two buildings, adorned by vases and benches, we cross the portico and go down to the **formal garden**, distinguished by *parterres* of box and citrus trees in *terra-cotta* urns.

Beyond a lawn slopes gently downward, inviting us to discover another part of the garden, built in tiered terraces.

A splendid stone stairway, of unusual polygonal shape, leads to the second level of the garden.

The composition is completed by a pool of water shaded by a majestic linden tree. A double ramp of stairs completes the layout of garden toward the countryside.

The path leads back to the villa skirting a great octagonal basin. With the two buildings now behind us, we cross the lawn to enter the *selvatico*. Before us are magnificent tiers of stone and another spectacular view. Two statues of women symbolizing *Spring* and *Summer* mark three avenues. The central one leads to the Zitti belvedere, opening onto the valley below, in the direction of Florence. This place is consecrated to silence and contemplation, and its name, which means "hush" or "quiet", derives from the attitude of the mysterious stone figures who seem to observe the visitor.

Lastly, a **column** expresses the gratitude of the workers employed by Caruso in reconstructing the park.

To know more

F. Borghini, *La Toscana di Caruso*, Florence 1998.

S. Bonavoglia, F. Parrini, *Mecenati e artisti in villa. Un patrimonio nascosto*, Lastra a Signa/Campi Bisenzio 1999.

Web: www.villacaruso.it

Poggio a Caiano
The garden of Lorenzo the Magnificent

fruit trees. On the eastern side, beyond the wall, was created a garden very similar in structure to that of numerous other Medicean gardens, divided by four crossing avenues and centered around the *boschet-*

HOW TO ARRIVE

In the center of Poggio a Caiano.
Address: Piazza de' Medici 14
tel.: +39 055 877012
fax: + 39 055 8796613
Visiting hours: Jan.-Feb., Nov.-Dec.
8:15 am - 4:30 pm; March 8:15 am-
5:30 pm; Apr.-May, Sept.-Oct.
8:15 am - 6:30 pm;
Jun.-Aug. 8:15 am-7:30 pm
Closed the 2nd and 3rd Monday
of the month, May 1, Christmas
and New Years Day
Free admission
Guided visits every hour
Accessible to the disabled
Restrooms

The side garden

E ncapsulated today by the town of Poggio a Caiano, the villa was built in a slightly elevated po-
sition. The effect is heightened by the solemnity of the building with its bastioned wall recalling the for-tified architecture of the past. It was just this sin-gular encircling wall that once enclosed a part of the 16th century garden now lost. The **villa** of Lorenzo the Magnificent was begun in 1485 to the project of Giuliano da Sangallo, but was still unfinished in 1492, the year of Lorenzo's death. In all probabili-ty no garden existed until the middle of the 16th cen-tury, when Cosimo I commissioned Tribolo and Da-vide Fortini, his son-in-law, to lay out the surround-ing area. A lunette by Justus Utens shows how the garden was divided into sections planted to dwarf

to for bird-catching. Of this garden, transformed be-tween 1819 and 1830 by Pasquale Poccianti, no trace remains today. Poccianti also built the *limonaia* and the cistern to collect water.

Entering from Via Pistoiese we cross the first gar-den with flower-beds of curvaceous shape and great cedar trees. From here there is a fine view of the villa embellished by its Della Robbian frieze. Many scholars believe it to be symbolically linked to the agricultural activity undertaken by Lorenzo at Poggio a Caiano. To the right of the villa a stair-way leads to the **garden** closed off on the southern side by Poccianti's huge *limonaia*. This garden, of very elegant form, has recently been embellished by flowers reviving the 19th century taste for color.

The villa

Continuing along the west side of the *limonaia* or returning to the level of the villa and descending the stairs behind it, we reach the 19th century *boschetto* with interesting trees.

To know more

M. Pozzana, *Il paesaggio, le ville, i giardini*, in "Antiche terre di Prato. Una nuova Provincia", Florence 1994, pp. 11-43.

Giardini Medicei, edited by C. Acidini, Milan 1996.

le Cascine
di Tavola

Not far from the Villa di Poggio a Caiano it is possible to visit (from the outside) the agricultural core of Lorenzo's property, the farm called Cascine di Tavola, a quadrangular building with four towers at the corners.

The complex was conceived in the 1470s as an experimental farm for raising cattle, producing cheese and planting various crops, such as rice.

The land was reclaimed and the waters of the Ombrone river channeled to resolve the problem of continuous floods.

Of the extensive transformation carried out in the 15th century, important traces remain today in the landscape. The broad straight tree-lined avenues still provide a pleasant place to walk.

Villa Casagrande
The garden of Marsilio Ficino

going on around it but linked to the urban villa, equipped with an olive mill and a great wine vat.

The history of the complex, consisting of a large building with an elegant cloister embellished with Ionic column capitals opening onto the **inner garden**, is closely connected to the Serristori family. Near the end of the 14th century, it was owned by

The garden towards the cloister

Enclosed by the high walls surrounding the historic centre of Figline Valdarno, the Garden of Villa Casagrande is the only example of its kind in the Valdarno.

In this serene, enclosed space that seems designed for meditation and reflection, it is easy to imagine Marsilio Ficino, who taught here, strolling amid the boxwood hedges and cypress trees. In reality, the garden was laid out and planted in the early 20th century, probably when the architect Giuseppe Castellucci restored the great building in neo-Gothic style at the request of Umberto Serristori.

Casagrande had been an important country estate for centuries, the centre of the agricultural activity

Ristoro di Ser Jacopo Serristori. Ristoro was a key figure in the history of Figline, having founded the famous hospital named for the Serristori family in 1399.

From the cloister we enter the enclosed garden. The walls built by the Florentines after having conquered Figline, between 1353 and 1375, form a barrier isolating the garden from the turbulent flow of traffic and everyday life just outside it.

In a great **tower** in the stone curtain wall, two broad arches open onto the garden. From this entrance we can appreciate the harmonious **geometry of the garden**, which may have been designed by Giuseppe Castellucci.

The geometrical garden

*Below:
the tower
in the medieval
walls of Figline*

The garden is divided into two parts. The central part is composed of four canonical sections separated by high boxwood hedges (some centuries-old box bushes can be seen from here), now kept as lawns. On the opposite side, on a lower level and separated by a broad boxwood hedge clipped in an original topiary cordon design, we descend to a lovely flower garden, where a group of tiny flowerbeds bounded by stone kerbs captivate the gaze with the beauty of their seasonal blossoming.

It is pleasant to pause in this serene space and recall the words of the writer Paul Bourget who, in regard to Casagrande and its garden, replied to a friend who had expressed the hope of spending spend much time in that place, capable of soothing the spirit: '*Dites plutôt qu'il serait bon d'avoir cet état d'âme qui vous permît de vivre ici ed d'y gouter la paix!!*'

To know more

Web: www.villacasagrande.it

Other gardens in Florence and around it

Giardino dell'Iris

Piazzale Michelangelo - Visiting hours: open from April 24 to May 20,
Visiting hours: 10:00 am.-12:30 pm, 3:00-7:00 pm - Free admission
tel.: +39 055 483112 (Società italiana dell'iris)
www.irisfirenze.it/giardino - segreteria@irisfirenze.it

The garden was created as site for the international iris show/competition held each year in spring.
A visit during the flowering season (April-May) is particularly interesting.

Giardino dell'Orticoltura

Via Bolognese 17 - Visiting hours: 8:00 am – 6:00 pm (seasonal variations)
Free admission - tel.: +39 055 2768752

Created by the Tuscan Horticultural Society in the mid-19th century, the garden is embellished by the iron and glass greenhouse designed by G. Roster, built in 1880. It has been a public garden since 1930.

I Collazzi

Via Volterrana 7, Scandicci, Florence - Privately owned. Visits not allowed.

The villa, attributed to Michelangelo, is preceded by a cypress avenue and surrounded by terraced gardens (the lower portion is a lemon garden).
The swimming pool is by Pietro Porcinai (1939).

Palazzo Medici Riccardi

via Cavour 3 - Visiting hours: 9:00 am – 7:00 pm - closed on Wednesday.
Admission: € 7,00; € 4,00 reduced
tel.: +39 055 2760340 - www.palazzo-medici.it

Created around the middle of the 15th century, the garden appears profoundly changed today. In the first two decades of the 20th century Enrico Lusini, commissioned by Arturo Linaker to redesign the garden, eclectically combined 15th century and Baroque elements.

Palazzo Vivarelli Colonna

Via Ghibellina 28 (entrance from via delle Conce)
Visiting hours: open Apr.-Oct. Tuesday and Thursday 10:00 am – 5:00 pm
Free admission - tel.: +39 055 2625940

Open only in particular circumstances, the garden is divided into geometric beds planted to box and has a *boschetto* of camellias on the eastern side. At the back of the garden is an 18th century wall-fountain.

Parco delle Cascine

From Piazza Vittorio Veneto to the Indiano Viaduct. Always open.

The park was given its definitive layout in the late 18th century. Interesting features designed by Giuseppe Manetti: the ice-house/pyramid and the two *tempietti*. At the western end, in 1865, the monument to an Indian prince was built.

Parco del Neto

Via Vittorio Emanuele, Calenzano - Visiting hours: winter 8:00 am – 5:00 pm,
closed on Monday; summer 8:00 am – 8:00 pm - tel.: +39 055 8874515

Fine examples of *taxodium* border the 19th century pond. The park originally belonged to Villa Gamba al Neto. Open to the public, it is now owned by the Municipality of Calenzano.

Parco Strozzi al Boschetto

Via di Soffiano 11 e via Pisana 77 - Visiting hours: winter 8:00 am – 8:30 pm (seasonal variations) summer and during events: 8:00 – 2:00 am
Free admission - tel.: +39 055 2767108

Park restored by Giuseppe Poggi around the middle of the 19th c. Interesting structures in Egyptian style.

Villa di Careggi

Viale G. Pieraccini 17 - Closed for restoration - tel.: +39 055 4382638

Medicean villa associated with Lorenzo the Magnificent. The original design of the garden can hardly be distinguished today due to the trees planted at later times. The *limonaia* and the grotto below the villa are interesting. A project for restoring both the villa and the garden is now in progress.

Villa Corsini a Castello
Via della Petraia 38 - Visiting hours: Sat.-Sun., 9:30 am – 1:00 pm
Free admission - tel.: +39 055 450752; guided visits: tel.: +39 055 234074
e-mail prenotazioni@cscsigma.it www.uffizi.firenze.it/musei/villacorsini

Recently restored, the villa, with its monumental Baroque facade, now houses a collection of archaeological finds that had been kept in storage at the Archaeological Museum for years. Passed from the Rinieri to the Corsini family in the late 17th century, it was transformed by G.B. Faggini, who created the garden of the Four Seasons and a French garden.

Villa Schifanoia
Via Boccaccio 121 - Visiting hours: by appointment only from Monday to Friday - Free admission - tel.: +39 055 4685338 - www.eui.eu

Italian garden commissioned by Myron Taylor in the 1930s; beautiful *parterre*. The villa is the site of the European University.

Villa Stibbert
Via Stibbert 26 - Visiting hours: Apr.-Oct. 8:00 am – 7:00 pm, Nov.-March 8:00 am – 5:00 pm; closed on Thursday; Free admission
tel.: +39 055 475520 - www.museostibbert.it - info@museostibbert.it

Park created in the second half of the 19th c. by G. Passeri and G. Poggi for Frederick Stibbert. At the center of the pond is an Egyptian-style *tempietto*; beyond, a *limonaia*. The villa, now a museum, houses the collections of its former owner. (The museum has different visiting hours from the park.).

Villa Il Ventaglio
Via Aldini 12 - Visiting hours: 8:15 am – 5:30 pm (seasonal variations)
Free admission - tel. and fax: +39 055 580283
www.sbap-fi.beniculturali.it - lia.pescatori@beniculturali.it

The park was created in the mid-19th century by Giuseppe Poggi. Important trees and broad lawns traversed by a carriage drive leading to the villa.

Villa I Collazzi

Parco delle Cascine, ice-house/pyramid

The garden of Villa Schifanoia

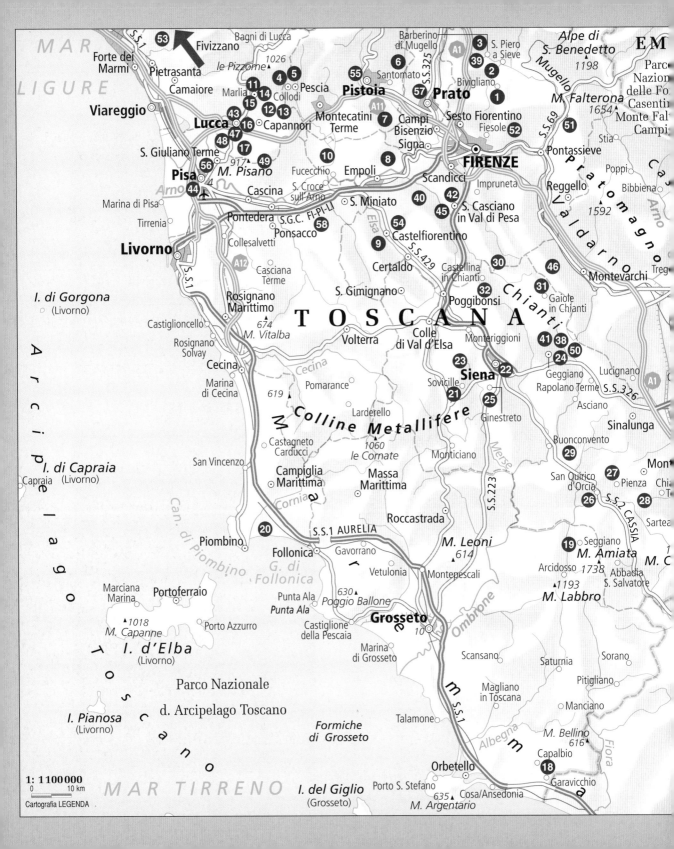

1407
.Fumaiolo

M. Carpegna
1415

Alpe
d. Luna

Pieve 1454 **MARCHE**
Stefano
Bocca Trabaria
1049

Sansepolcro

Città di
Castello

zo 1082
M. Favalto

astiglion
orentino

Cortona
33

Pergo
34

Lago
Trasimeno

Perugia

no

Chiusi

U M B R I A

L. di
Corbara

apendente

A1

di

na

Montefiascone

Z I O

Viterbo

In Tuscany

1 Villa di Bivigliano	98	
2 Castello del Trebbio	100	
3 Castello di Barberino di Mugello	102	
4 Parco di Pinocchio	104	
5 Giardino Garzoni	106	
6 Parco di Celle	110	
7 Villa La Magia	114	
8 Villa Bibbiani	116	
9 Giardino di Granaiolo	118	
10 Villa il Castelluccio	120	
11 Villa Marlia	122	
12 Villa Mansi	128	
13 Villa Torrigiani	130	
14 Villa Buonvisi Oliva	134	
15 Villa Grabau	137	
16 Palazzo Pfanner	140	
17 Villa Massei	142	
18 Giardino dei Tarocchi	144	
19 The garden of Daniel Spoerri	146	
20 Parco della Sterpaia	148	
21 Villa Cetinale	150	
22 Villa di Vicobello	154	
23 Castello di Celsa	156	
24 Geggiano	160	
25 L'Apparita	162	
26 Horti Leonini	164	
27 Giardino di Palazzo Piccolomini	166	
28 La Foce	167	
29 La Ragnaia di S. Giovanni d'Asso	170	
30 Castello di Brolio	172	
31 Badia a Coltibuono	174	
32 Fonterutoli	176	

33 Giardino Passerini	178
34 Il giardino Reinhardt	180
35 Villa Sandrelli	181
36 Parco Tommasi Aliotti	182
37 Villa Guillichini	183
38 Castello di Belcaro	184
39 Castello di Cafaggiolo	184
40 Castello di Montegufoni	184
41 Certosa di Pontignano	184
42 Le Corti	184
43 Orto botanico di Lucca	184
44 Orto botanico di Pisa	184
45 Poggio Torselli	185
46 Roseto botanico Carla Fineschi	185
47 Torre Guinigi	185
48 Villa Bernardini	185
49 Villa Borrini	185
50 Villa Gori Muratori Ginanneschi	185
51 Villa di Gricigliano	186
52 Villa I Busini	186
53 Villa La Pescigola	186
54 Villa di Meleto	186
55 Villa Puccini	186
56 Villa Roncioni	186
57 Villa Rucellai	186
58 Villa Varramista	186

Villa di Bivigliano
A 17th century woods

HOW TO ARRIVE

Near Bivigliano,
reached by a brief detour from
Via Bolognese.
Owner: the Pozzolini family
Address: Via del Viliani 84,
Bivigliano, Florence
Bus: SITA-AMV line 306
tel. and fax: +39 055 4067717
Guided visits: by appointment
only at Associazione Culturale
Akropolis (tel. +39 055 461428)
Partially accessible to the disabled
Restrooms

The first level of the garden consists of four beds of box with a lovely **fountain** in the center. The second level is an exquisite orchard, recalling the 16th century tradition of orchards in the Medicean gardens. Below appears a modern *pergola*.

The fountain in the formal garden

A broad lawn flanked by cypresses stands before this beautiful villa, of Buontalenti influence. To its left is the elegant chapel dedicated to the Madonna of the Snow. The building, with a formal terraced garden, was constructed in the early 17th century by the Ginori family. The most fascinating element of the estate is the great woods extending for over 12 hectares. Created in the 17th century, it was transformed by the Pozzolini family, who became its owners around the middle of the 19th century.

On the left of the building we enter the **formal garden**. Composed of two terraces, it is situated to the south, facing on the valley that overlooks Florence. The gaze sweeps over an enormous landscape, bounded on the right by the monumental **cypress avenue**.

The natural scenery surrounding the garden is the wooded, mountainous one of the Mugello, and it may have been the local features of the landscape to suggest the creation of the woods, a real hunting park planted at the wish of Filippo Ginori near the end of the 17th century (1690).

The woods, situated beyond the access road, are traversed by a broad, straight avenue that slopes gently down to a rustic **grotto** built of stone. The grotto, surmounted by a terrace with balustrade, is reached by an inner winding staircase (an inscription on the right records the year it was built: 1690). Before the grotto a vast circular space, surrounded by majestic trees, calls to mind other theatrical areas in the garden.

During the 19th century the woods was enriched by an interesting collection of conifer trees, including over one hundred examples of sequoia and tuje which have found an ideal environment in the damp climate of the Mugello.

To know more
Web: www.villadibivigliano.it

The cypress avenue

The grotto in the park

The front of the villa

Castello del Trebbio
The origins of the villa garden

HOW TO ARRIVE

North of Florence,
in the vicinity of San Piero a Sieve.
Owner: Lorenzo Scaretti
Address: Via del Trebbio 1,
San Piero a Sieve, Florence
tel.: +39 340 4987306
e-mail: info@y-knot.net
Visiting hours: by appointment
only for groups (max 40 persons).
Admission fee to be established
upon booking the visit,
guided visit included
Poorly accessible to the disabled
Bookshop

ing from 1434, the year when the Medici's exile was revoked and they were called back to the city. It thus seems probable that it was Cosimo himself who commissioned Michelozzo to renovate the castle. In 1451 Trebbio passed to the secondary branch of the Medici family. Lastly, in 1936, it was inherited

The grapevine pergola

A typical Medieval construction built on the crown of a hill, the Castello del Trebbio offers a splendid view over the Mugello landscape. Transformed into a modern residence by Michelozzo di Bartolomeo around the middle of the 15th century, the castle has never entirely lost its original aspect of fortress. It boasts an extraordinary **garden**, a rare example of *hortus conclusus* preserved intact over the centuries and still today recognizable in its main elements. Giovanni di Bicci came into possession of Trebbio in 1386. After Giovanni's death in 1428, his property passed to Cosimo and Lorenzo; and already in 1428 Cosimo began to invest in the Mugello region. This policy was pursued more energetically start-

by the Scaretti family through a complex series of transitions. And it was with Marjorie Jebb Scaretti that the final transformation of the house and garden took place.

The finest feature of the garden is its splendid **pergola**, repeatedly imitated and reiterated in the construction of 20th century gardens. It has 46 columns of Michelozzian influence built of brick with sandstone capitals either *a foglie d'acqua semplice* or with fluting. Sixty-nine grapevines (*Vitis vinifera*) climb up the columns to form a green, living roof. The architectural features that distinguish the Michelozzian garden appear remarkably innovative. Almost prefiguring the plan that was to become characteristic of the villa garden, one of the first gardens conceived to ornament a castle was created. On the right side of the castle is the orchard, structured in three terraces. The first terrace is entirely occupied by the pergola while the second is instead a real orchard. The second terrace originally held another *pergola*, now lost. The use of terraces in laying out the garden recalls the farm terracing used to cultivate steep hilly lands, a custom that was molding the Tuscan agricultural landscape already by the 14th century and that became widespread in the 16th century. In front of the house, where the lawn with the 'green pavilion' represented in a lunette by Justus Utens (1599) is located, Marjorie Webb Scaretti has designed a simple formal garden with sections planted to box and roses. On the right appears a rock garden of typically English taste, adjacent to the wall of the house; further to the right is a grove of fruit trees. At the back, sheltered by a backdrop of cypress trees, is a lawn and an area set aside for outdoor games. Lady Scaretti, in collaboration with her son Lorenzo, has supplemented the cypresses that surround the house, planted by the Philippine Fathers in 1820 and by Austrian prisoners of war lodged in the castle in 1917. In the area of the *pergola* and the lower terrace the 20th century alterations were more limited, consisting only of the creation of a double hedge of cypress with borders of roses and lavender. The *pergola* has remained unchanged and the orchard still has the pool and the sections planted to *erbaggi,* or herbs, appearing in the lunette by Utens.

To know more

Giardini Medicei, edited by C. Acidini, Milan 1996.

Web: www.y-knot.net

The garden near the castle

Castello di Barberino di Mugello
An open-air theater

The wisteria pergola

steep slope (almost 25 meters difference in altitude). The problem was resolved by creating a system of terraces buttressed by traditional stone walls. In 1924 Giulio Coronati, in describing the garden "in 15th century style", found it "abounding in laurel, cypress, myrtle and other evergreens, with pergolas of roses of every variety and splendidly flowering espaliers". The visitors' admiration shows how Socini's garden represents a highly successful revival of the 15th century Tuscan garden.

The layout of the garden presents very particular features, appearing as an enormous triangle, the tip turned toward the town and the base toward the castle. The eastern side bounded by a monumental cypress avenue and a pergola, the western side by another *pergola* and the woods. The garden is thus distinguished by two very long **pergolas**, originally of roses, later of grapevines and now of **wisteria**.

Three distinct parts can be observed. Below the castle is the 'garden theater', followed by garden rooms of box with cypress and ilex trees, and last an orchard and a vegetable garden between the two pergolas. The various parts are arranged hierarchically according to a canon theorized and applied already in the 16th century (a canon which, in later times, was always observed in designing formal gardens). The ornamental garden is placed close to the building while the orchard and the other productive

From the center of Barberino di Mugello the castle and its garden are not visible today, since thick vegetation conceals the construction in spite of its dominating position. The Medieval castle, built by the Cattani family around the year One Thousand, remained their property for many centuries. It was transformed into a manor house in the 15th century, when its military and defensive functions had become obsolete.

After the castle had passed from Leopoldo Cattani to the Manelli Galilei Riccardi family, in 1915, it was bought by Luigi Dapples, who transformed the villa and embellished it with a large garden, commissioning the project of the architect Agenore Socini. Laying out the hillside in front of the castle could not have been an easy task for Socini, considering its parts follow and are connected to the *selvatico,* to the *ragnaia* for bird-catching and to the farm landscape. The **ornamental garden** is interpreted as a black-and-white garden, that is, without flowers, rhythmically marked only by the compact volume of the hedges and the vertical soaring of cypress and ilex. The central sector, containing a pool of water, is composed of four sections of box with cypress trees and small **statues**.

Itinerary of visit

Descending from the castle, we find on the right the ***teatro di verzura,*** or garden theater, situated at the center of a group of tall trees in homage to the traditional Italian garden. Four tiers of turf, marked off by spheres of box, form benches for the spectators. The rectangular stage is enclosed by a hedge of laurel surrounded by cypresses.

Above: the formal garden

Bottom: a statue in the garden

In the lower part of the garden is the orchard, divided into six sectors. Numerous fruit trees grow here, apples, pears, plums and apricots in particular. From the orchard there is a fine view of the imposing castle with its towers and crenellations.

The complexity of the garden's geometric design and the harmonious linking of the parts reveal the great ingenuity of its designer, and even suggest the possibility that Socini may have received help from another, perhaps a foreign landscape artist.

Returning to the courtyard of the castle we find a small rose garden, closed off by a pergola. A central bed of sinuous profile frames two monumental cedars. Adjacent to the castle is a large park. It may have been Luigi Dapples himself, together with his brother, who decided to plant numerous conifers. In the vicinity of the garden theater in particular grow fine examples of *Sequoia sempervirens, Abies alba, Abies pinsapo,* and *Cedrus atalantica* var. *glauca.*

To know more

M. Pozzana, S. Salomone, *Il castello di Barberino di Mugello,* Florence 1999.

Parco di Pinocchio
A fairy-tale told by nature

The whale in the Collodi Park

stages and involved different artists. First to be built
was the area where the *Red Shrimp Tavern* and the
Laboratory of Words and Figures are found today.
Then the *Land of Toys* was completed, designed as
a garden itinerary along which statues are placed
to illustrate the major episodes in the story of Pinocchio. Nature, ingeniously modeled by the landscape
artist Pietro Porcinai, thus fully participates in the
adventurous life of Collodi's marionette.
Contrasting with the elegant simplicity of the first
portion of the park, inaugurated in 1956, is the elaborate modulation of the land distinctive of the second part, rich in botanical varieties, inaugurated in
1972; covering a little over one hectare, it has been
conceived as a space divided into two sections
bounded by a great avenue of ilexes. Three artificial hillocks create the illusion of a space larger than
it really is.

Itinerary of visit

The entrance to the garden is located beside the *Red
Shrimp Tavern*. After crossing the lawn with the statue of the *Good Fairy, Pinocchio and the Dove* by
Emilio Greco, we find on the right a little square laid
out like a checkerboard and the building of the *Laboratory*; in front of it, a woods of tall ilexes trimmed

The *Pinocchio Park* is the only example in Italy
of a park created to illustrate a fairy tale using
art, with a natural itinerary marked by the sculptures of contemporary artists.
The construction of the park, linked to the name of
Rolando Anzilotti, took place in two successive

in geometric shapes encloses the *Piazzetta of mosaics* by Venturino Venturi. Within the woods is a playground for children and a number of resting places with wooden benches and tables. At the end of the woods a paved path leads to the *Land of toys* ('Paese dei balocchi').

We then enter Pinocchio's *Village* with the imposing figure of the **Carabiniere** by Pietro Consagra standing ready to bar the way. Continuing along the path, built of stones from the ancient streets of Pescia, we climb the first of the three artificial hillocks to find the *Talking Cricket* and the *Marionette Theater*. From here on the vegetation assumes a different aspect. Leaving behind us clipped hedges of ilex, we enter a *boschetto* of chestnuts and Scotch pines with an underbrush of typically Mediterranean shrubs.

At the crest of the hill is the *Tavern of the fox and the cat*. From here, descending along a path bounded by hedges of cane apple, we note on the left a little olive grove that calls to mind Pinocchio's flight through the fields in search of his two friends.

On the right the vegetation now becomes a dark woods concealing the figures of the *Assassins* who, in Collodi's story, hang Pinocchio to an oak tree. Further on we come upon a clearing in the woods where, in an open, luminous space, the *Child Fairy* stands surrounded by flowers.

At the end of a little valley covered with sweet-smelling roses appears the *House of the Good Fairy* with the bedroom where Pinocchio was treated by the three doctors; outside is the *Snail*.

Continuing up another slope that leads to the *Gold coin tree* we find the frightening *Serpent* coming down a path bordered by high walls of laurel and ilex. At the top on the left the *Grown-up Fairy* stands on a little hill; at the bottom of the hill are the *Rabbits carrying a coffin*. Beyond a *boschetto* of bamboo are the *Crab* lying in wait, ready to spray water on visitors, the *Fishnet* and the *Frying Pan* of the green fisherman, and lastly the *Circus* with Pinocchio transformed into a donkey.

Suddenly, around a sharp curve, appears a magnificent view of the pond with the **Whale**, its enormous mouth gaping wide open. Inside the whale is *Geppetto*, carrying the *Blue goat* on his back.

Lastly Pinocchio, now become a real child, greets visitors inviting them to enter the adventurous world of the pirates, on their ship, in the *Treasure cave* and in the mysterious *Maze*.

To know more

A. Massa, *I parchi museo di scultura contemporanea*, Florence 1995.

Web: www.pinocchio.it/pinocchio

The Carabiniere *by Pietro Consagra*

Giardino Garzoni
Mazes and waterworks

HOW TO ARRIVE

Not far from Pescia,
take the Chiesina Uzzanese exit
from highway A11.
Privately owned.
Address: Piazza della Vittoria 1,
Collodi, Pistoia
tel: +39 0572 427314
e-mail: giardinogarzoni@pinocchio.it
Visiting hours: Mar.-Oct. every day
from 8:30 am to sunset;
Nov.-Feb. Sat.-Sun. from 9:00 am
to sunset (excepted groups making
reservation).
Admission: 13,00 €,
reduced 10,00 € (3-14 years old,
over 65 and groups of at least
20 persons), 9,00 € for schools;
Free admission for under 3
Guided visits: +39 0572 490919.
(The ticket includes The Collodi
Butterfly House)
Restrooms
Café - Restaurant
Bookshop

an indivisible whole with the little town. In the first half of the 17th century Romano Garzoni laid out a garden consisting of a broad area in the shape of an amphitheater. From here, along the slope, a path leads to terraces immersed in a wood of ilex. The garden is completed by a pond, the little painted chapel of the *romitorio*, a great ilex woods and three terraces where citrus trees grow along espaliers.

Garzoni also created, in the area of the four terraces adjacent to the palazzo, an aviary, a flower garden,

The 'garden theater'

The Garzoni garden and villa form a stately, imposing whole. In addition to conserving the last 17th century maze remaining in what was once the State of Lucca, it also boasts a 17th century *parterre de broderie* of exquisitely French taste. Furthermore, its position on a steep hillside (45 meters of difference in altitude) makes this estate unique. The hillside rises so steeply before the village of Collodi as to form

and the maze with its grotto. In what is now a *boschetto* of bamboo he placed an orchard with a variety of plants. In the second half of the 18th century a second Romano Garzoni, bearing the same name as the first, transformed the enclosed garden by creating an itinerary in a symbolic/esoteric key. He converted the ancient *romitorio* into the building of the Banetti and added the statue of *Fame*. He enlarged the pond and embellished it with decoration; created a lovely water chain with statues and rocailles; changed the 17th century grotto into a cistern providing water for the *giochi d'acqua* of the fountains below, and built the new grotto of *Neptune*.

Lastly, he constructed the '**garden theater**' and the little theater of Pomona. During this same period a *parterre* designed according to French taste was added in the amphitheater area. Garzoni also worked on the Palazzina dell'Orologio behind the villa, built according to the indications of Filippo Juvarra.

The entire system of 17th - 18th century gardens has remained unchanged up to the present day, apart from some 19th century replacement of vegetation. After 1842 in fact, Giuseppe Garzoni converted the orchard into a *boschetto* of bamboo, added the palm trees along the avenue of the second terrace and made some changes in the avenue of the Emperors.

Itinerary of visit

The first view of the garden appears from the little square in front of the gate, purposely created in the 17th century to provide a broad perspective panorama. Only from here is it possible to observe the perfect harmony between garden and palace, and to discover the anamorphic mascaron half-hidden by the rocailles of the **water stairway**.

The entrance opens onto a broad area in the form of an amphitheater, affording other views of the garden. Tall cypress hedges serve as frame to a group of statues that presage the symbolic messages appearing along the main path through the garden: *Flora, Diana,* the *Fauns, Bacchus* and *Ceres, Apollo* and *Daphne.* This area is distinguished by the *parterre de broderie* as well as by two imposing jets of water in the circular basins. In front, in the sloping *parterre*, appears the Garzoni coat of arms, surrounded by hedges of box and little flower beds framed by the paths.

The majestic stairway

Avenue of Emperors

Statue of *Fame*

Chain of waterfalls

Stairway
with grottoes

Garzoni
Coat of Arms

*The garden in an early 20th
century photograph*

Above are the thick supporting walls of the three terraces. Adorned with espaliers of citrus trees, they stand out against the complex interwoven ramps of the central stairway. The different levels are marked by large niches placed on the same axis. The first niche holds the **fountain** of the **Contadino**, or peasant, pouring water from a barrel. He is flanked by four small niches with the statues of the *Seasons*. The second niche forms an arch leading to the grotto of Neptune, an octagonal area lined in *spugne* with a fountain and waterworks. In the upper niche is the fountain of the *Villano*, or peasant. He is surrounded by a group of small statues representing monkeys playing ball and two dogs, supplementary elements of the garden's symbolic program. Above this structure the statues of the two *Satyrs* frame the scene appearing further up: the great 'water chain' with the statue of *Fame* at its top. This part of the garden, called the *Avenue of Emperors,* is perhaps the most striking feature of the park.

At the top of the water stairway is an avenue of camellias with four oriental sofas and a statue of the *Turk.*

The decoration of the pond, which can be clearly observed from this point, shows obvious cracks created by the designer to represent the effects of an earthquake. It is in fact from the shaking of the earth that the statue of *Fame,* blowing water into the pond below, emerges.

A number of garden paths lead up the hill to the building of the Bagnetti, where the Garzoni family once bathed to music played by a chamber orchestra.

To the left of the avenue of camellias is a gate opening onto a path leading to the palazzo. We then cross the *Ponte sul Rio* with its waterworks controlled from the flower garden above, adorned with the fountains of *Hercules with the Hydra and Sampson slaying the Philistine.* From the bridge the works in the maze below can be actuated.

We are now in the avenue of the Poor. To the right a gate marks the private area of the garden; to the left a path leads down to the maze with the grotto and to the *boschetto* of bamboo.

From here a narrow wooden bridge returns to the enclosed garden.

After passing the fountain of the Wild Boar we follow the path along the outer edge of the garden to reach the **garden theater** with its statues of *Comedy* and *Tragedy.*

From here we can take the narrow, half-hidden paths lying between high cypress hedges back to the level part of the garden and the amphitheater.

The rustic grotto with the statue of the Contadino

To know more

F. Gurrieri, *Il giardino e il castello Garzoni a Collodi,* Collodi 1975.

J. Chatfield, *A Tour of Italian Gardens,* New York 1988.

V. Cazzato, M. Fagiolo, M.A. Giusti, *Teatri di verzura. La scena del giardino dal Barocco al Novecento,* II ed., Florence 1995.

Web: www.pinocchio.it/giardinogarzoni

Parco di Celle
An encounter with environmental art

HOW TO ARRIVE

Near Santomato,
along the Via Pistoiese.
Owner: The Gori Collection.
Address: Via Montalese 7,
Loc. Santomato, Pistoia
fax: +39 0573 479486
e-mail: goricoll@tin.it
Visiting hours: May – September
(closed in August and on holidays)
only upon presentation of request
in writing (for instructions, see the
website)
Restrooms
Bookshop

The Villa of Celle, an imposing Baroque structure, is surrounded by a scenic garden from the same period, consisting of a flower garden and a great orchard of fruit trees. All around, for 25 hectares, extends the 19th century park, arriving as far as the slopes of the distant hills.

The site is magnificent, and nature is bountiful. It may have been this enthralling atmosphere that inspired Giovanni Gambini, commissioned by the owner Caselli around the middle of the 19th century, to lay out an extensive romantic park and furnish it with an aviary, a tea pavilion, a lake and an *orrido*, or waterfall, according to the Central European fashion of the times. The destiny of the park thus seemed marked. Here, where the power of nature is so magic and so strong, it was only natural that environmental art should emerge as the dominating theme.

The contemporary park was created by Giuliano Gori,

Katarsis
by Magdalena Abakanowicz

Labyrinth *by Richard Morris*

Formula Compound *by Dennis Oppenheim*

the present owner, a highly cultured collector.

In the early 1980s Celle received the first works of artists who wanted to display their production outdoors, rather than in the restricted space of museums and galleries. Some of the property used as farmland was then subjected to other initiatives, aimed at allowing the surrounding nature to be perceived from a different viewpoint.

A visit to the park is always guided by experts who work with the collection. Significant moments in the history of gardening are discussed, harmoniously interwoven with the viewing of works of contemporary art, extraordinary and versatile. Around many of the works are places of pause that recall the *fabriques* of French 18th century parks: garden furnishings that become architectural spaces and gardens within a garden.

Labyrinth by Richard Morris (1982), a work in Trani stone and serpentine in two-tone bands, recalls the style of Tuscan Romanic churches. Placed on a gentle slope, it invites the visitor to explore it and experience the sense of bewilderment it inevitably evokes. From a nearby platform the maze can be seen from above, with its triangular plan and inner meanders.

Theme and Variations II by Fausto Melotti (1981) is one of this great sculptor's most important works. We find it near the little lake in the vicinity of the villa. Eight steel elements six meters high bear chains, spheres and other elements that, moved by the wind, produce sounds of mystic resonance. The shape mirrored in the

Above: Celle Sculpture *by Mauro Staccioli*
Bottom: My hole in the sky *by Bukichi Inoue*

water and the sounds emitted link the work to the surrounding environment in a kind of symbiosis. Between the lake and the tea pavilion the American sculptress Beverly Pepper, exploiting the concave morphology of the terrain, has created a work of art that is midway between sculpture and architecture, **Celle Theater Space**, dedicated to Pietro Porcinai. The stage ends in two backdrops made of cast iron covered with turf, in an installation that is a sort of outdoor theater. The triangular tier of seats, ending at the top in two cast iron columns recalling the shape of a diapason, can hold 350 persons.

Between 1985 and 1989 the Japanese artist Bukichi Inoue built a symbolic itinerary entitled **My hole in the sky** and installed it along the edge of the park, in the olive grove. From a square piazza a trickling channel of water invites us to traverse a long corridor between two walls of stone. Halfway down the corridor the path is barred by little basin of water. Continuing we enter, according to the artist's intention, the "viscera of the earth", from which we exit by climbing a winding staircase built of white marble. On returning to the surface we find ourselves standing in a glass cube.

Jan Hamilton Finlay, an artist and poet who has created many works linked to the garden, chose to position his poetic *Virgilian woods*, created in 1985, outside of the park; little sculptures in bronze appear beside a plow, a basket of fruit and some inscriptions hanging from the branches of the olive trees. Recently the Japanese artist Hidetoshi Nagasawa has constructed a zen garden in yellow marble. It is situated beyond a fountain inserted in the corner beside the entrance to the environment/installation.

To know more

G. Gori, *Introduzione a Arte Ambientale*, Turin 1993.

VV.AA., *Arteopenduemilasei. Itinerari possibili*, Trieste 2007.

G. Colette, *L'artiste contemporain et la nature: parcs et paysages europeens*, Paris, 2007.

Web: www.goricoll.it

My hole in the sky *by Bukichi Inoue*

artifice
and nature

Just beside the waterfall an epigraph records the work of Giovanni Gambini: "in the years '44 and '45 of the 19th century / this rocky cliff having been built above/the thick wall... / Gio.Gambini of Pistoia, requested to decorate this part of the wood, having completed the island / and the borders of the lake, imagined it, directed it / and without the devices used by art / made it conform to lovely nature / showing itself more original and severe". These words express all the philosophy of the art of romantic gardens: creating "conforming to nature", that is creating works that appear wholly natural even when they are produced by ingenuity, and are therefore artificial.

Celle Theater Space *by Beverly Pepper*

"If foreseeing the future is a risky game in which man tends by nature to participate, for the collection of the Celle farm we can risk some optimistic predictions based on the deep-rooted presence of its installations, on the programs now being carried out and on the availability of new and ample spaces. The most comforting indications come however from those who, for natural reasons of consanguineous succession, will follow in our footsteps, because they too feel growing within them the same needs and the same curiosity that have urged us in the past to take the most beautiful path from among the many that form the maze of life".

Giuliano Gori, *Introduzione a Arte Ambientale*, Turin 1993

Villa La Magia
From hunting park to art park

family's financial ruin. This major purchase clearly shows how the grand-ducal house intended to extend its holdings in this territory, ideal for hunting. Already by 1585 work had begun on building an artificial lake connected by a road to the villa, as can be seen in the lunette by Utens depicting the villa

The lemon garden bordered with rose hedges

surrounded by orchards and gardens, with the great forest behind it. At the centre of the lake, on an artificial island, stood a little building used for hunting birds of passage. The villa lies at the centre of the Poggio, Artimino, Ambrosiana and Montevettolini hunting reserves, Medicean villas that gravitate around the 'Barco Reale' of Montalbano, which had been created by Cosimo I expressly for hunting.

Bernardo Buontalenti was commissioned to remodel the property. Presumably, he also worked on the villa, which was enlarged by towers built at the corners, a typology commonly found in the fortified residences of the Medici.

No further changes were made until 1645, when the villa was sold to Pandolfo Attavanti, who remodelled its interior without changing its outer proportions. Attavanti created the system of gardens that

Villa la Magia, situated in a dominant position above the Ombrone Valley, overlooks the peaks of Montalbano in the vicinity of Quarrata. Its ancient place name derives, it seems, from a Pistoian noblewoman, 'Mona Magia', (according to Emanuele Repetti), although many other hypotheses have been advanced.

In early 1584 Francesco I dei Medici bought the medieval-style building that had been constructed by the Panciatichi family in the 14th century, when the property was sold at auction consequent to the still today surround the villa, and commissioned Giovan Domenico Ferretti to decorate the interior with frescoes. In 1766 the property was sold to the Amati family from Pistoia. It remained in their possession until only a few years ago, when it was bought by the City of Quarrata, which is now implementing a major project of contemporary art installations, some of them already been completed, such as Nagasawa's labyrinth and Poirier's installation near the lake; Daniel Buren's fountain is now being installed.

The garden is canonically laid out on two levels. The first consists of the great lawn surrounding the villa. The second, reached by descending the original **monumental staircase** built in the early 19th century, is the **lemon garden**, divided into geometric sectors.

The garden retains the baroque layout seen in Giuseppe Zocchi's print dating from 1744, where it appears already architecturally completed, situated on a terraced level below the villa.

Bitter orange trees grow espaliered against the wall, and the lemon garden to the south opens out toward Montalbano. The six sectors bordered with flowers or little hedges (now rose hedges), dwarf fruit trees, and a *parterre de broderie* in the four central sectors surrounding the **big round basin** built in the first two decades of the 18th century, are clearly apparent in the print. The lemon garden today is enclosed on both sides by lemon houses. We know that after the middle of the 18th century the big lemon house to the west, built in the late 17th century, was enlarged, and new stables were added by Bindaccio and Leone Ricasoli, relatives of the Attavanti family. After the Amati family purchased the property, work on the exterior contin-

Above: the fountain and the villa

Bottom: the staircase between the lawn and the lemon garden

ued, most notably with the construction of the lemon house to the east. In 1792 Antonio Gamberai received payment for designing a duct that brought water to the garden, where the irrigation system composed of little canals and basins for collecting water in the vicinity of the lemon trees still exists today. Gamberai also worked to transform the woods to the east into a romantic little park, in keeping with the new fashion for English landscape gardens. The park was also given a beautiful brick entrance designed in elegant neoclassical style (built after 1797).

To know more

C. Barni, *Villa La Magia. Una dimora signorile nel contado pistoiese secc. XIV –XIX*, Florence 1999.

Web: www.villalamagia.com

Villa Bibbiani
A fascinating botanical collection

HOW TO ARRIVE

Between Florence and Empoli,
Montelupo exit from
the Firenze-Pisa-Livorno highway.
Owner: Paola Giovanna Donato
Del Gratta and Donatella
Marchiafava Del Gratta
Address: Loc. Bibbiani,
Capraia, Florence
tel.: +39 0571 57338
a-mail: bibbiani@timenet.it
Visiting hours: by appointment
only for groups of at least 10
persons (May-September)
Guided visits
Admission: 10,00 €
Partially accessible
to the disabled
Restrooms
Bookshop

using them for both ornamental purposes and forestry could thus be verified. Ridolfi began to occupy himself with the park at the desire of his mother Anastasia, who was particularly interested in developing it. As he wrote in 1843, "I find in the care related to such a pleasant duty a pastime that is both delightful and instructive, to which I abandon myself with passionate commitment. My dearest studies seem even sweeter to me amid the

The formal garden

impenetrable brush that I am transforming into flowery woods". In short time the garden became famous for its botanical collections. Some of the plants were grown outdoors (particularly interesting are the collections of *Crataegus*, *Eucalyptus*, *Ficus*, and *Magnolia*), some in greenhouses and tepidarium, such as the fine examples of *Cactus* and *Pelargonium*. A role of special importance in Ridolfi's collections was played by camellias (the garden's first catalogue lists a remarkable 195 species or varieties of camellias) and araucarias. From an araucaria seed sent to Bibbiani by the horticultural establishment Budin of Chambéry was grown a plant recognized by the famous botanist Pietro Savi as belonging to a new species. It was called *Araucaria ridolfiana* in homage to Ridolfi.

An austerely elegant building, its appearance softened only by the graceful **formal garden** on the southern side, Villa Bibbiani owes its fame to the great park in which it is immersed, one of the most important gardens of acclimatization in Italy (along with those of Villa Hanbury at Ventimiglia and Villa Ricasoli on the promontory of the Argentario).

In the park, planned by the famous statement and agronomist Cosimo Ridolfi, numerous botanical species coming from different climates were planted in the early decades of the 19th century. Their capacity for adapting to Italian weather and the possibility of

The formal garden

The park, which may have been designed by Ridolfi himself, covers nearly 20 hectares. Winding paths lead through clumps of brush and sun-lit clearings. The visitor discovers the numerous botanical species still existing today in an alternation of views typical of the 19th century sensitivity for landscape.

The feeling of a romantic park is accentuated by the *fabriques* scattered through the garden, the little buildings that adorn it: the ice-house, the furnace and the arch of Man, an imitation ruin.

The formal garden dates from the early years of the 20th century. It houses a graceful 'garden theater' divided into *parterres* of evergreen shrubs and embellished by topiaries and exotic palms.

The collector's tradition harking back to Ridolfi lives again today in the nursery of exotic conifers, where 27 species of rare pines of great ornamental value are grown.

Chronology

15th c. Bibbiani is the feud of the Frescobaldi family.
1809 Anastasia Frescobaldi asks her son Cosimo, statesman and agronomist, to "render pleasant this estate of Bibbiani, which she loved, how much she could not say, as a paternal keepsake".
1843 Marchese Cosimo Ridolfi publishes the *Catalogo delle piante coltivate a Bibbiani e cenni su qualcuna delle medesime*, listing the numerous species of herbs, shrubs and trees, both exotic and domestic, existing on his property.
1903 The estate is sold to Baron Raimondo Franchetti, who purchases other farms in the direction of Pulignano and gives particular impetus to wine production.
1937 Bibbiani is bought by the Del Gratta family, who are its present owners.

To know more

G. Moggi, L. Falciani, *Guida botanica al parco di Bibbiani*, Florence 1991.

F. Chiostri, *Parchi della Toscana*, Todi 1989.

Web: www.bibbianifattoria.it

Giardino di Granaiolo
A courageous initiative

HOW TO ARRIVE

Between San Miniato and Certaldo, along S.S. 429.
Owner: The Pucci family
Address: Loc. Castelfiorentino, Florence
Visiting hours: by appointment only (at the owner's discretion).
Information: L.P. Studio srl, Via dei Pucci, 6 Firenze
tel: + 39 055 2399201

The tiered lawn

The building as it is today, an imposing parallelepiped surmounted by a central tower, probably results from successive renovations carried out by the Pucci family, the long-time owners of the estate. The most recent initiative, dating from 1970, was the work of the architect Gae Aulenti.

The garden appears today of an extreme simplicity. It is formed of a series of **low tiers of turf** bounded by stone curbs. The earthen tiers widen out in front of the villa, modeling the gentle slope before it. This is not only a conceptual revival of the terraced or tiered garden of Tuscan tradition, but also an innovative interpretation that manages to frame the classic construction of the villa in a geometry harmoniously fitted into its context.

Behind the house a flower border represents the only concession to color in a project that is based on the essential, and is a remarkably early anticipation of avowedly minimalist themes.

The original project called for the construction of a swimming pool surrounded by a high wall, to the side of the villa. The wall was not built however and the pool appears today as a simple rectangular basin inserted among the trees of the park.

As recalled by Gae Aulenti in a brief text written sixteen years after the Granaiolo project, the new garden took the place of the existing layout in Italian garden style.

"At the turn of the century", recalls the architect, "there had been constructed in front of the house, surrounded by vegetation in the form of *macchia*, an Italian garden with palms, shrubs and fountains that had impaired the harmonious relationship". The new design for the garden was thus a bold initiative, evidently intended to reconstruct a lost harmony and equilibrium through a decided and to some extent daring gesture that can be seen today as anticipatory. Aulenti adds, "I designed the Tuscan garden of Granaiolo in 1970, and every time I visit it or see it again in a photograph I am amazed that it exists. How it is possible that intelligent persons such as my clients believed in the drawings I presented them enough to decide to build that garden?".

This doubt, retrospective, sprung from an awareness of the difficulty of designing a garden destined to change and evolve over the course of time. How was it possible to predict the metamorphosis of a park designed in the severest, strictest geometry into something natural and harmonious? "For myself as well", concludes Aulenti, "although I foresaw the possibility, it was hard to believe in it, so much so that I can today tranquilly declare the risk and definitively decide that I will never design another garden". The original idea of the designer was that of "applying the principle of Land Art, an art that penetrates into the earth, that impresses on the earth the sign of an expression, and this without repudiating the long tradition of the Italian garden". Granaiolo thus represents the successful attempt to give shape to an idea, to transcribe the signs of Land Art in the form of a welcoming, comfortable garden, inhabited daily. It is also the entirely concrete proof that one can learn from what exists and skillfully utilize an ancient lesson, integrating it into a language of innovative content.

To know more

G. Aulenti, *Un progetto mediterraneo*, in O. di Collobiano, O. Camerana, I. Origo, G. Aulenti, "Altri giardini, altri orti", Milan 1986.

The villa

Villa
il Castelluccio
A contemporary masterpiece

The lawn
in front of the house

HOW TO ARRIVE

Not far from Empoli, the Empoli
or Santa Croce sull'Arno exit
coming from the Firenze-Pisa-Livorno highway.
Owner: Antonella Catastini Covini
Address: Via dei Medici 6,
Ponte a Cappiano, Fucecchio,
Florence
Visits at the owner's discretion,
to be previously agreed with Pietro
Porcinai Association, via e-mail to:
segreteria@associazioneporcinai.org

In the countryside between San Miniato and Fucecchio, in the nearby between the cities of Florence and Pisa, around a fine 17th century construction standing on the crest of a little hill, Pietro Porcinai created one of his most mature and complete works in the years between 1971 and 1980.

Thanks to the understanding and collaboration of exceptional clients Porcinai was challenged to express his talent by designing an entire portion of landscape, remodeling the terrain, providing a pond for irrigation, and lastly creating a whole woods.

The design is structured around a long grassy ring road that runs around the hill halfway up, set off by groves of trees, thickets of shrubs and flowering slopes. Within the ring is the garden proper, in close contact with the house. The entire complex includes a swimming pool covered by an iron-and-glass structure, a tennis court placed in a natural amphitheater, a greenhouse and a parking area with garage.

Itinerary of visit

Along a path through the woods we arrive at the gate to the estate. In traversing an avenue of olive trees we find two box hedges clipped in the shape of pilasters, marking the entrance to the **lawn** surrounding the house.

The parking area is on the left, embellished by an ingenious play of paving in stone and pebbles alternating with patches of lawn. In front of the villa the lawn is softly modeled. From here the gaze sweeps over the countryside, and the domesticated landscape drifts off into the natural one around it, framed by a hedge of pomegranates.

Concealed by box shrubs are skylights over the swimming pool below. A splendid **path** leads to the area of the swimming pool, flanked by a silvery escarpment of *Teucrium fruticans* and a mixed hedge of laurel and cane apples. Upon entering the garden, beyond the large sliding door that closes it off, we can admire the perfection of the details, the materials and the colors. The tones are the restful ones of wood and terra-cotta, along with the green of ferns, *Ficus,* papyrus and *Ruscus.*

The pool is splendid, especially for the contrasting colors of various materials: black ceramic tesserae on the bottom, white pebbles on the walls. The service areas, for which Porcinai designed the furnishings, link the level of the swimming pool to the house through the basement. Further on, through a glass door, we arrive at the greenhouse; on the lawn stands **a bronze sculpture** by Primo Conte.

Returning to the house we walk through a clump of field maples, blazing with color in autumn.

On the lowest terrace appears a grove of poplars, a subtle reference to the surrounding landscape. Descending still further we reach the grassy path that runs round the hill; still lower appears an artificial lake around which have been planted reeds, willows, elms and sorbs.

In autumn the bright red of the *Taxodium distichum* stands out in vivid contrast to the white tones of the poplars.

Above: the ring road
Bottom: the entrance to the villa

To know more

M. Matteini, *Pietro Porcinai architetto del giardino e del paesaggio*, Milan 1991, pp. 202-208.

VV.AA., *L'eclettismo nell'opera di Pietro Porcinai*, edited by T. Grifoni, Florence 2006.

Villa di Marlia
An enchanting landscape

HOW TO ARRIVE

Not far from Lucca,
take the Altopascio exit coming
from highway A11 (Firenze-Mare)
Owner: the Pecci Blunt family
Address: Marlia, Lucca
tel.: +39 0583 30108
e-mail: info@parcovillareale.it
Visiting hours: only for groups by
appointment from December
through February. From March
through November guided visits
every hour from 10:00 am to 1:00
pm and from 2:00 pm to 6:00 pm
Closed on Mondays (unless holiday)
Admission: 7,00 €, reduced 6,00 €
(for groups of at least 20 persons).
Poorly accessible to the disabled
Restrooms

The latter villa, surrounded by an important garden with nymphaeum, bears on the door the Bernardino Guinigi coat of arms (1723-1729).

The park, inserted in a magnificent landscape, covers 19 hectares and is divided into three gardens, each dating from a different period - the Baroque garden

The villa seen from the lake

The park of the royal villa of Marlia is the most important in the Lucchesia and its complex history of numerous transformations and stratifications makes it extraordinarily interesting (the villa is still today called "royal" because after having been owned by the Grand Duke of Tuscany it became the residence of Vittorio Emanuele II King of Italy).

Within the park are three constructions: Villa Buonvisi Orsetti, around which has been created a remarkable Baroque garden; the 18th century Palazzina dell'Orologio, on the same axis as the great *ragnaia* of the first garden; and Villa del Vescovo, now uninhabited, built in the 16th century over an existing structure owned by the Archbishop of Lucca.

around the villa and the Palazzina dell'Orologio; the romantic park; and the *art deco* garden laid out in the 1920s.

The Baroque garden, with its imposing *ragnaie*, water theater and *teatro di verzura*, is harmoniously linked to the symphony of colors distinctive of the landscape portion, abounding in rare and exotic plants. Contributing to the striking effect of the whole is the garden of Jacques Gréber, created in the early 20th century according to the model of the Islamic water garden.

Itinerary of visit

The Baroque garden surrounds the villa in a harmoniously linked pattern of separate sectors. From the exedra at the entrance we arrive at the long rectangular lawn from which the villa appears in all its elegance. Continuing to the left we enter the avenue that leads through the ancient *ragnaia*, formed of high hedges of laurel and ilex; at the end of the avenue appears the lovely facade of the **Palazzina dell'Orologio**.

From the avenue through the *ragnaia*, to the right, a beautiful gate leads to the **lemon garden**. It is divided into four sectors, each of them framing a great magnolia tree.

To the south the garden is closed off by a niche with fountain. To the north a semicircular ramp of stairs

The garden theater

leads to the ornamental **fishpond** with statues of the rivers *Arno* and *Serchio*; at the end is a lovely nymphaeum with a **statue of *Leda and the Swan***. In homage to Leda, a pair of swans lives in the rectangular pool.

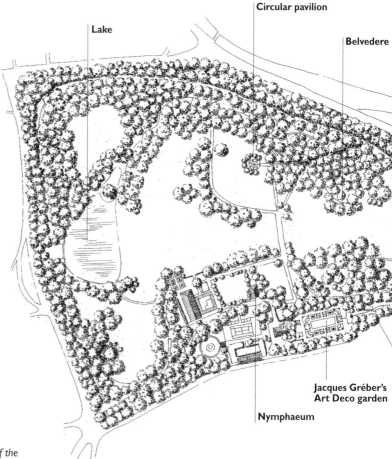

Above:
detail of the
atrium in the
nymphaeum

Bottom:
the modern garden
by Jacques Gréber

detail of the water
theater

Through a circular garden room with waterworks and fountain, a path transverse to the fishpond leads to the *teatro di verzura*. Built of yew and box, it is designed like a real theater. At the back of the stage, three terra-cotta statues of *Colombina*, *Pantalone* and

Balanzone pay homage to the tradition of the *Commedia dell'Arte*.

From the fishpond we return toward the villa. Behind the building a broad semicircular basin marks the boundary of the garden while linking the park and villa to the hills in the background.

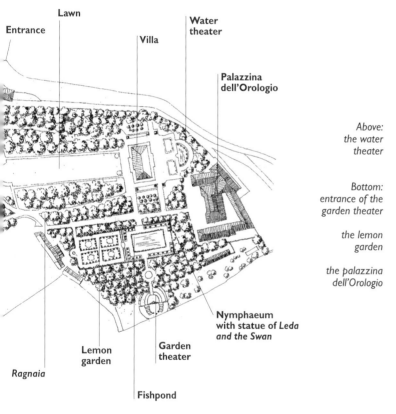

*Above:
the water
theater*

*Bottom:
entrance of the
garden theater*

*the lemon
garden*

*the palazzina
dell'Orologio*

The **water theater**, a vivid Baroque scenario of water, stone and vegetation, is a recurrent element in the villas of the Lucchesia. The nearby Villa Grabau as well as Villa Oliva have similar features, designed to confer greater solemnity on the space.

The fishpond; in the background, the fountain with the statue of Leda and the Swan

Enlarging the property by purchasing the nearby Villa del Vescovo, Elisa Baciocchi managed to create one of the finest 19th century parks in all Tuscany. Favored by the beauty of the site, the rich soil and the climate itself, the unknown designer of the park (undoubtedly influenced by the ideas expressed by Jean Marie Morel in the treatise *Théorie des jardins*, published at Paris in 1776), skillfully harmonized the existing formal gardens with the new romantic park. The alternation of irregular lawns, of open and closed areas, creates a varied scenario that concludes with the **lower lake**, from where there is the best view of the villa. In autumn the blazing colors of the great red oaks, the beech-trees, the tulip trees and gingko offer an unforgettable spectacle. On the left, climbing the slope, we find a modern circular pavilion entirely surrounded by a pergola of wisteria.

Continuing beyond the hillock/belvedere, created to afford a view of the park from above, we can admire the extraordinary flowering of the camellia woods. On the right is the Villa del Vescovo, erected on a monumental base with niches and statues. The formal garden was renovated at the turn of the century. The 16th century **nymphaeum** appears as a splendid pavilion preceded by a loggia. Entirely decorated in grotesque designs, the nymphaeum is composed of an atrium with terra-cotta and pebble flooring and an octagonal room with vaulted ceiling, where three niches hold

Detail of the topiaries near the villa

fountains adorned by sea gods.Returning from the nymphaeum to the villa, on the right we reach an area of the park transformed in the 1920s.

Here the French landscape artist Jacques Gréber created a games area with an unusual swimming pool and a **formal garden** inspired by Islamic water gardens, according to the *art deco* style then in vogue. The garden, rectangular in shape, seems carved out of the surrounding vegetation and is distinguished by brightly colored plants and flowers. Hedges of *euonimo*, with their yellow-green leaves, contrast with brightly flowering hibiscus and bougainvillea.

The bougainvillea plants are dug up and moved to the greenhouse each year, to be planted outdoors again in springtime. This practice, complicated and expensive, clearly shows the demanding and refined nature of Gréber's project.

To know more

Architetture del verde. Le Ville gentilizie lucchesi e il loro territorio, edited by M. Vannucchi, Lucca 2000.

Web: *www.parcovillareale.it*

Chronology

16th c. The villa is built by the Buonvisi family.
1651 After the bankruptcy of the Buonvisi, the villa passes to the Orsetti family. The garden is renovated in Baroque style.
1805 Elisa Baciocchi, Napoleon's sister, becomes the sovereign of Lucca. She creates the romantic park with the acquisition of the Villa del Vescovo and its gardens. The twin pavilions are created on the piazzale with exedra at the entrance.
1918 Sold by the Borbone family, the villa becomes the property of the Pecci Blunt family.

Villa Mansi
Baroque waterworks

HOW TO ARRIVE

In the vicinity of Capannori,
near the Capannori exit from highway
A11 (Firenze-Mare)
Owner: San Michele Society, Pistoia
Address: Via delle Selvette, 242,
Segromigno in Monte, Capannori,
Lucca
tel.: +39 0583 920234
fax: + 39 0583 928114
Visiting hours: every day except Monday,
10:00 am – 1:00 pm, 2:00 pm – 5:00 pm
in Winter; 10:00 am – 1:00 pm,
3:00 pm – 6:00 pm in Spring
and Summer
Admission: 3,50 €, reduced 2,50 €
(for groups of at least 7 persons),
free admission for students, over 65
and under 12

initiative that remains today is the '**water chain**', which runs through the length of park, flanked by hedges and statues of human or animal figures.

The chain of little waterfalls ends in the broad octagonal basin that was the fulcrum of Juvarra's design. The formal *boschetto* was in fact planted in the shape of a star radiating out from with the little square containing the basin.

From here the water flowed on to a **fishpond** of elegant design decorated with balustrades and statues. Georg Cristoph Martini (1685-1745), a guest at Villa Mansi, described the area around the fishpond in his *Viaggio in Toscana*: "Near the palace, on the right hand, is the so-called fish-

The 'water chain'

The boschetto *of banana trees behind the villa*

The park of Villa Mansi was built in successive eras. The harmony with which the various initiatives have been carried out over the course of time has resulted in an ensemble of unique beauty, containing a vast range of plant species.

In the 16th century the garden was first laid out with terraces and geometric beds extending around the villa. The Renaissance park was then transformed in the 18th century, probably by Filippo Juvarra.

The only feature of the 18th century

pond where fish are kept, into which statues personifying the rivers pour water. Around the pool run magnificent paths lined with hedges and a majestic walk between great elms and other trees.

I slept in a chamber that opened just onto this *boschetto*, and listened all night to the exquisite music of the nightingales that nest there in great number".

Beside the basin, in the direction of the villa, once stood the secret garden, a space isolated by a wall where flowers blossomed in geometric *parterres*.

The visual fulcrum of the garden was the 'Bath of Diana', a pond with an imitation ruin with statues of the goddess of hunting and a swimming water-nymph. As a result of the 19th century transformation of a portion of the garden into an English park, the Bath of Diana is now isolated within a *boschetto*.

Other additions made during the Romantic period include the broad lawn in front of the villa that heightens the effect of the imposing residence. The splendid facade should be observed from a distance, at the top of the gently sloping lawn, surrounded by romantic woods and brightened in autumn by the colors of the *Liriodendrun tulipifera*.

Surrounding the lawn is the **romantic woods**, where some exotic species grow (*Cedrus atlantica*, *Picea abies*, *Pseudotsuga menziesii* and *Chamaecyparis lawsoniana*).

On the eastern side of the villa is a path lined with palm trees and a *boschetto* of bamboo. To the west of the building is a fine collection of camellias containing many rare varieties.

To know more

A. Brilli, *Viaggiatori stranieri in terra di Lucca*, Milan 1996 (the quotation form Georg Cristoph Martini is on p. 97).

The fishpond

Villa Torrigiani
The garden of Flora

HOW TO ARRIVE
Not far from Capannori,
the Capannori exit from highway
A11 (Firenze-Mare).
Privately owned.
Address: Via Gamberaio 3,
Camigliano, Santa Gemma, Lucca
tel. and fax: +39 0583 928041
e-mail: villatorrigiani@villeepalazzi-
lucchesia.it
Visiting hours: 10:00 am – 1:00 pm,
3:00 pm – 6:00 pm
from March to October;
from June to September
closing time at 7:00 pm.
Free admission for under 12,
guides and tourist accompaniment
Guided visits
Accessible to the disabled
Restrooms

The garden of Flora

A majestic **avenue of ancient cypresses** leads to the magnificent villa standing in a fine position at the foot of the hills. In this part of the Lucchesia a splendid succession of villas and gardens forms a landscape unique the world over for elegance and beauty.

The original plan of the garden dates back to the 16th century, when the Buonvisi family owned the estate. In the first half of the 17th century the new owner Nicolao Santini, ambassador from Lucca to the court of Louis XIV, transformed the garden, inspired by the splendor of French style.

In 1816 the villa becomes property of the Torrigiani family, after the marriage between Vittoria Santini and the marchese Pietro Guadagni Torrigiani.

Some 18th century *cabrei*, or maps, illustrate the Baroque layout, often attributed to the hand of Le Nôtre, although certain documentation is lacking. The elegant design of the *parterres* and the broad stretches of water in front of the villa and behind it reveal the strong influence of French taste.

The Arcadian poet Filandro Cretense (pseudonym of Antonio Cerati), after visiting the villa, described the garden in his *Ville lucchesi*, published in 1783: "a most pleasant lawn, crowned with green espaliers, opens at the end of a broad road lined with cypresses, providing a fine horizon to the facade of the palace. On the opposite side appears an atrium beyond which stretches an exquisite garden; and two fountains at the same distance share the honor of embellishing the uniformity of those flourishing plains".

Remaining from the 17th century garden are the two great pools on the lawn before the villa, the **garden of Flora** and the nympheaum, or Grotto of the Winds, to the right of the main building. The Baroque garden is structured along an axis that includes the fishpond above and the garden of Flora, a rare example of Baroque flower garden, on the lower level. The two levels are connected by a system of stairways adorned with statues and vases. The Garden of Flora can be entered by passing behind the villa and then descending, or by entering directly from the garden level and then climbing a stairway leading to the top of the fishpond. A lovely area adorned with flowers is bounded by walls and enhanced by the geometry of the beds planted with hedges and spheres of clipped box. To the south the garden ends at the nymphaeum, an octagonal pavilion with a dome crowned by the statue of *Flora*, decorated with wrought-iron masks and flowers. In the nymphaeum the waterworks were once so spectacular as to induce Filandro Cretense to praise hydraulics, the science that allowed such marvels to exist. In the niches stand seven statues of the *Winds*.

The side garden in the spring flowering season

Above:
the villa

Bottom:
the upper pool

the avenue
of cypresses

**17th century
basins**

Entrance

The splendid pavement of black and white pebbles, with its spiral pattern, is striking. A portion of the Baroque garden was replaced by the 19th century park. The variety of the trees is remarkable, in particular for the majestic *Liriodendron tulipifera*, the tulip tree, and the so-called bald cypress (*Taxodium distichum*). The collection of camellias is also important for its 19th century varieties.

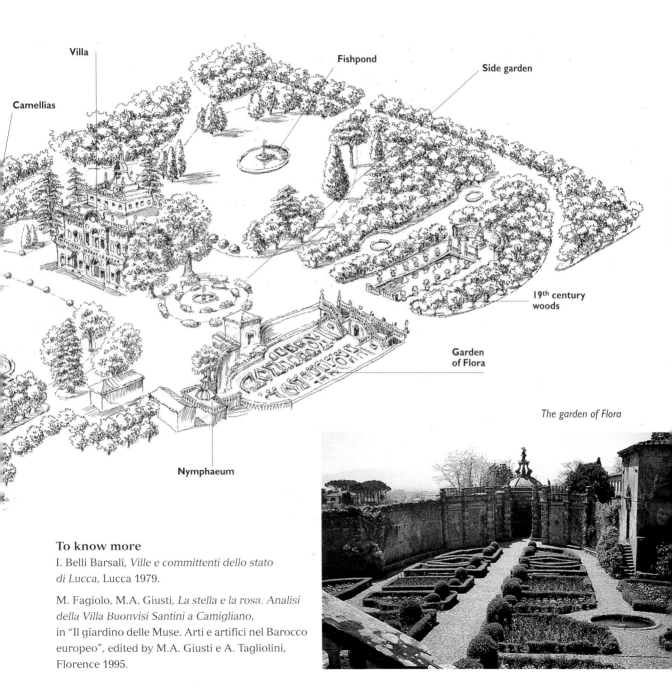

Villa

Fishpond

Side garden

Camellias

19th century woods

Garden of Flora

The garden of Flora

Nymphaeum

To know more

I. Belli Barsali, *Ville e committenti dello stato di Lucca*, Lucca 1979.

M. Fagiolo, M.A. Giusti, *La stella e la rosa. Analisi della Villa Buonvisi Santini a Camigliano*, in "Il giardino delle Muse. Arti e artifici nel Barocco europeo", edited by M.A. Giusti e A. Tagliolini, Florence 1995.

Villa Buonvisi Oliva
Water music

for a transverse connection realized through the 'water chain' of the *Cascatelle*.

To the right of the avenue, supported by a grassy escarpment, is the formal section of the park, originally divided into regular beds (no longer distinguish-

HOW TO ARRIVE

In the vicinity of Marlia, Lucca or Capannori exit coming from highway A11 (Firenze-Mare)
Owner: Luisa Oliva
Address: San Pancrazio, Lucca
tel.: +39 0583 406462
e.mail: info@villaoliva.it
Visiting hours:
9:30 am - 12:30 pm, 2:00 pm - 6 pm from March 15 to November 15.
Visits are possible by appointment also in the closing time.
Admission: 6,00 €
Free admission for under 12

The backdrop of ilexes

The garden that surrounds Villa Oliva at San Pancrazio, celebrated in the 18th century by Filandro Cretense (pseudonym of the Arcadian poet Antonio Cerati), elegantly reiterates many elements typical of the gardens surrounding the Lucchese villas.

The mansion, standing in a dominant position north of the weir, is the fulcrum of a composition organized around the main axis of the long entrance avenue. To the left of the entrance extends the agricultural area, destined to the cultivation of fruit trees and vineyards. It is laid out in a system of terraces rising toward the villa, which was originally the center of an economic organization based on agriculture. At Villa Oliva, the garden structure is particularly interesting; the system of terraces is not parallel, but rather perpendicular, to the facade of the villa. This gave rise to the need

able today due to the 19th century transformations). This section contained the *boschetto*, the *ragnaia* and the garden proper. The compact volume of the villa, of austere late 16th century style, opens at the back, toward the hillside, through a magnificent portico facing on a broad semicircular space. This exedra, an element often found at the end in many Lucchese villas, is planted to lawn and bordered by potted citrus trees. The curved background, formed of a **compact hedge of ilexes**, opens at the center to show a rustic grotto decorated with calcareous concretions, stalactites and tufa.

The Baroque plan of the garden has remained unaltered and the 19th century changes are superimposed on the original structure, which can still be distinguished. Today the villa is embellished by a collec-

*The waterfalls
before the pool
of the* Amorini

*The statue
of the* Pitocco

tion of tall trees, in the 19th century Lucchese style: monumental cedars, magnolias, gingkos and horse chestnuts.

Itinerary of visit

A visit to the garden starts from the side entrance with its two monumental decorated pillars (in front of the parking lot). We find ourselves behind the villa that opens onto the grandiose loggia by Matteo Civitali. Framing the great elliptical lawn with the fountain of the Angel is a **backdrop of ilexes** that blends harmoniously with the hills behind it, with a rustic grotto at its center. We continue toward the beautiful stables, now used for ceremonies, up to the modern swimming pool. On the parapet is a terracotta **statue of the** *Pitocco*.

Upon arriving at the villa we find opening out before us an extraordinary network of gardens laid out on three different levels - the upper level with its *boschetto* of ilexes and pool surrounded by flower beds, a section that was transformed in the 19th century; the central level with a long avenue of ilex and cypress leading to the main entrance, the **pool of the** *Amorini*, the **fountain of the** *Cascatelle*

The fountain of the Siren

and the *Kaffeehaus*; last comes the lower level, with the gallery of hornbeams and the farm area. The fountain of the Cascatelle is the first of three fountains placed along the 'water chain'.

The other fountains, placed in the wall encircling the weir, are the fountain of *Abundance*, not far from the *limonaia*, and the splendid **Fountain of the Siren**, surmounted by the coat of arms of the Buonvisi family.

To know more

I. Belli Barsali, *La villa a Lucca dal XV al XIX secolo*, Rome 1964.

I. Belli Barsali, *Ville e committenti dello stato di Lucca*, Lucca 1979.

Giardini e parchi lucchesi nella storia del paesaggio italiano, edited by A. Maniglio Calcagno, Lucca 1992.

Web: www.villaoliva.it

"It [the garden] is situated on a broad rise so that there extends before it a most lovely perspective of lakes, rivers, woods, hills and populated villages, which things Nature with seductive disorder reunites, forming so to say an immense gallery of animated pictures".

Filandro Cretense,
Le ville lucchesi, 1783.

The garden in front of the villa

Villa Grabau
Trees play the leading role

Great trees
in the park

HOW TO ARRIVE

In the vicinity of Marlia, Lucca
or Capannori exit coming from
highway A11 (Firenze-Mare)
Owners: Francesca and Federico
Grabau.
Address: Via di Matraia 269,
San Pancrazio, Lucca
tel. and fax: +39 0583 406098
e-mail: info@villagrabau.it
Visiting hours: from Nov. 2 to March 31
only on Sunday, 11:00 am - 1:00 pm and
2:30 pm - 5:30 pm; from April 1 to June
30 and from Sept. 1 to Nov. 1 every
day 10:00 am - 1:00 pm and 2:00 - 6:00
pm; from July 1 to August 31 every day
10:00 am - 1:00 pm and 3:00 - 7:00 pm.
Closed on Monday morning.
Visits are possible only for groups and
by appointment during the closing time.
Admission: 5,00 € for the park, 7,00 €
for the park and villa, reduced 6,00 €
Reductions for under 16 and groups
(min 10 max 40 persons).
Groups over 40 persons: 5,50 €
Accessible to the disabled
Restrooms - Bookshop

Villa Grabau appears at the end of a long avenue leading from the fine gate marking the entrance to the property. The garden, covering an area of nine hectares situated on a plain at the foot of the Pizzorne hills, was created in successive stages and is surrounded by farmland.

The villa has been owned by the Grabau family since 1868. Built in late Renaissance style presumably near the end of the 16th century (as replacement for a pre-

vious Gothic building), it was renovated in neo-classic style in the 19th century. Arriving at the villa by a ring path running around the lawn, we pass through halls frescoed with fine *trompe l'oeil* designs to arrive at the back, where the main perspective axis is further developed and refined. Here we find the formal garden, laid out in two levels separated by a stone balustrade decorated with mosaics and fountains. On the upper level, along the borders of two great lawns, stands the collection of lemon trees. At the back a circular fountain and a backdrop of ever-

The villa seen from the entrance

The garden furnishings

greens conceal the entrances to the *selvatico*. The splendid Baroque wall/fountain separating the two levels is built of local Matraia stone and white marble and is decorated with rock crystal, foundry materials, quartz and tufa. Four bronze masks emerge from the wall, spouting water into four semicircular pools. The design, elegant and expressive, has led art historians to attribute the satyrs' heads to Pietro Tacca, one of the finest interpreters of Florentine Mannerism. The second level of the garden is reached by climbing the little stairway in the center of the wall, guarded by a pair of marble dogs.

In front of the villa extends the English park created in the 19th century, probably in two successive stages. Known for its important botanical collection, the romantic garden has a *boschetto* of bamboo, a *Montagnola* or hillock, and a great circular lawn that enhances the view of the villa. The collection of exotic conifers and broad-leaf trees offers a scenario of re-

The limonaia, *exterior*

placed at the center of the circular fountain in the formal garden, it represents a tortoise, the animal sacred to the god Pan, bearing a dragon with a human head and a mask at the back.

On the eastern side of the formal garden is the winter greenhouse; on the western side, the **limonaia**. Recently restored, the *limonaia* provides shelter in winter for the over 100 lemon trees in the park. It has a splendid facade, with seven rustic work portals and seven oval windows standing out against the Pompeian red of the plaster. Inside the building is a wall fountain with the head of Bacchus and a table listing the precise locations of all of the citrus plants to be sheltered during cold weather. On the western side of the villa is a 'garden theater' in boxwood.

markable beauty, especially in autumn. Two great red beech trees, to the right of the villa, cover the lawn with a carpet of bright leaves. On the left conifers and a great tulip tree form a variegated backdrop. Within the woods, in the northern part, a strange grotesque figure carved in stone stands in a clearing. Formerly

To know more

I. Belli Barsali, *La villa a Lucca dal XV al XIX secolo*, Rome 1964.

Giardini e parchi lucchesi nella storia del paesaggio italiano, edited by A. Maniglio Calcagno, Lucca 1992.

Web: www.villagrabau.it

The limonaia, *interior*

Palazzo Pfanner
The garden of the four elements

The garden looking toward the palazzo

HOW TO ARRIVE

At the center of Lucca.
Owners: The Pfanner family
Address: Via degli Asili 33, Lucca
tel.: +39 0583 954029
(tourist information city hall of Lucca
tel.: +39 0583 583150
fax: +39 0583 991667)
Visiting hours: every day from April
1 to October 31, 10:00 am - 6:00 pm
(with seasonal variations)
Admission: for villa and park 4,00 €
(5,50 € for villa and park), reduced
3,50 € (4,50 e for villa and park)
for children 12 to 16, over 65, groups
of at least 10 persons, students
Free admission for under 12
Accessible to the disabled
Restrooms

Near Piazza San Frediano in Lucca, set like a jewel between the bastions of the walls and the 18th century palazzo, is a splendid Baroque garden abounding in statues and fascinating views. The beauty of the whole was undoubtedly one of the reasons why the director Jane Campion decided to shoot some of the outdoor scenes for her film *Portrait of a Lady*, taken from the book by Henry James, on the premises of this villa.

The central section of the garden is arranged along the perspective axis indicated by statues of divinities and mythological heroes. On either side of the entrance, in two niches, stand the statues of *Cybele* and *Hercules*. At the center is an **octagonal pool** with the statues of the *Four Elements*: Vucan represents Fire, Mercury is the symbol of Air, Dionysus of Earth, Oceanus of Water. In the background, along the city wall, runs the long *limonaia* now abandoned, its elegant brick facade rhythmically broken by great windows alternating with laurel hedges. At the center of the facade two lions flank a basilisk, the emblem of the Controni family. Although the garden at first sight appears as a *hortus conclusus,* in reality the interior space is always in contact with the tree-lined wall of the city and with the urban fabric as a whole.

In the second half of the 17th century the Moriconi family undertook the construction of the palace and began to lay out the garden. Toward the end of the 17th century the Controni family, who had become the owners of the property, embellished it with the construction of the splendid exterior stairway.

With its system of arches and balustrades, the stairway provided a new scenic backdrop.

In 1860 the property was bought by Felice Pfanner, an industrialist of German origin who built a beer factory there, which was to remain open until 1929. The garden was included in the production facilities, and was used for beer tasting (both palace and garden still belong to the Pfanner family).

Itinerary of visit

The garden can be approached from two different directions; either by walking along the path on top of the city walls and suddenly discovering it beyond the Abside of San Frediano, or by passing through the doorway in Via degli Asili opening in a severe facade that gives no hint of the marvels concealed behind it. The half-shadow of a deep portico opens out into the garden with its statues.

At the center of the path is an octagonal pool in masonry, partially modified by the rock garden beds placed next to the main body. The pool, surrounded by a wide border of box, is equipped with an interesting hydraulic system (the circular underground basins can still be seen). The other section of the garden is formed of broad lawns thickly scattered with potted lemons; some still bear the date 1843. Along the sides of the formal garden are tall hedges of laurel and box and two *boschetti* of bamboo originating in the 19th century.

To know more

Lucca segreta. Giardini e orti della città murata, edited by M. Vannucchi, Lucca 1997, pp. 142-143.

Web: www.palazzopfanner.it

The fountain at the center of the garden

Villa Massei
A Garden in Lucca

HOW TO ARRIVE

Not far from Lucca,
taking the Capannori exit
from highway A11 (Firenze-Mare)
Owners: Gil Cohen and Paul Gervais
Address: Via della Chiesa 53,
Massa Macinaia, Lucca
fax: +39 0583 90138
e-mail: info@agardeninlucca.com
Visiting hours: only for groups
by appointment
Guided visits
Not accessible to the disabled

*The villa
and the great
camellia*

Although dreams only rarely come true, the one of Paul Gervais and Gil Cohen has done so: to live in a villa with a magnificent garden at the gates of Lucca. In a book dedicated to Villa Massei Paul Gervais recalls his splendid adventure. The villa is a 16th century hunting lodge that once belonged to Count Sinibaldi. Almost austere in design, the building is embellished by the loggia behind it, newly opened and restored. The modern garden was created by its two owners from Boston starting in 1982. Over the existing structure of the formal garden, containing a nymphaeum and a series of terraces descending along the sides of the entrance road, they have created a succession of garden rooms.

The lawns at the sides of the road are sprinkled with lovely wild flowers. In the lawns, divided by channels filled with water, are collection pools revealing the interesting hydraulic system that was undoubtedly responsible for the agricultural prosperity of the area. The entrance avenue leads to the villa. In front of the

elegant brick-red facade an **ancient camellia tree**, on the right, bears witness to the importance of the plantations that once stood in the garden. The effect of the building is heightened by a broad flower-bordered lawn where greens and whites alternate in exquisite harmony.

The owners experiment with new plants and different methods of growing them. On the northern side of the villa, around the doorway, is a green arch created with the delicate foliage of the *Muelenbeckia complexa*. On either side of the doorway are vases covered with the drooping foliage of *Buxus hallendii*. A late Victorian rose that flowers abundantly, 'La Follette' climbs over the nearby trees.

New gardens planned with sensitivity and intelligence fill the existing spaces, presenting a vegetation so rich as to form a true botanical collection.

The rose garden, an area of transition leading to the garden rooms, is splendid for its fine collection of antique roses (such as the perfumed 'Cuisse de Nymphe Emue', the red 'Cardinal de Richelieu' and the pink 'Souvenir de la Malmaison') alternating with modern roses produced by the famous English nursery of David Austin. Outstanding among the garden rooms are the one dedicated to the Italian garden, laid out by

A geometric parterre

Paul Gervais with sixteen beds of box and plantings of 'Heavenly Blue' *Caryopteris x clandonensis.*

The garden has recently been enlarged by building a long **pergola** supported by brick columns, enclosed in high hedges. At the end of the *pergola*, a leaping spray of water in the circular basin placed serves as eye-catcher.

The pergola

The garden has also been embellished with new furnishings designed by the owner. Near the swimming pool is the Mediterranean garden, where every two years the *Geranium maderense* comes into bloom. Before a little building is a formal garden surrounded by rosemary hedges. Botanical curiosities of modern taste alternate with memories from the past; for example, the great camphor tree with its perfumed leaves bears witness to the 19th century fashion for exotic plants, widespread in the Lucchesia area. The magnificent tree dominates the space behind the villa, where the nymphaeum is framed by a pergola of wisteria. The composition is completed by hydrangeas of various species and a border of peonies.

To know more

P. Gervais, *A Garden in Lucca,* New York 2000.
P. Gervais, *Un giardino a Lucca,* Schio 2008.
Web: www.agardeninlucca.com

Giardino dei Tarocchi
A game or a philosophy of life?

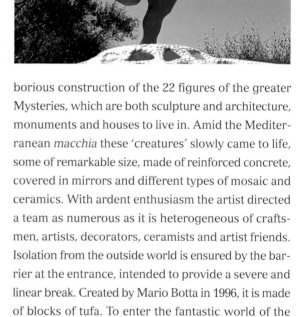

Card n. XIIII
Temperance

HOW TO ARRIVE
Between Capalbio and Garavicchio,
Chiarone exit in the direction of Pescia
Fiorentina coming from S.S. I Aurelia.
Owner: Fondazione
Il Giardino dei Tarocchi
Address: Garavicchio, Capalbio,
Grosseto
tel.: +39 0564 895122
E-mail: tarotg@tin.it
Visiting hours: from April 1
to October 15, 2:30 pm - 7:30 pm
By appointment only and upon
presentation of request in writing
for groups of at least 15 persons
at other seasons
Admission: 10,50 €, reduced 6,00 €
(under 12, over 65, students)
Free admission for the disabled
and under 7
Accessible to the disabled
Restrooms - Bookshop

Niki de Saint Phalle had been trying for years to make a dream come true: to create a garden that would hold all of the personage and places of the tarot cards, become the symbol of her artistic and existential life.

Within the space of an old stone quarry owned by the Caracciolo family, against the background of the Maremma landscape where Tuscany borders on Lazio, her dream became reality in the years between 1979 and 1996. The park came to life through the laborious construction of the 22 figures of the greater Mysteries, which are both sculpture and architecture, monuments and houses to live in. Amid the Mediterranean *macchia* these 'creatures' slowly came to life, some of remarkable size, made of reinforced concrete, covered in mirrors and different types of mosaic and ceramics. With ardent enthusiasm the artist directed a team as numerous as it is heterogeneous of craftsmen, artists, decorators, ceramists and artist friends. Isolation from the outside world is ensured by the barrier at the entrance, intended to provide a severe and linear break. Created by Mario Botta in 1996, it is made of blocks of tufa. To enter the fantastic world of the tarot cards visitors must confront this barrier, passing through the great circular opening.

Many of the figures can be penetrated, walked over or even lived in, as in the case of the great sphinx that represents the *Empress*. Within its capacious belly, lined by thousands of fragments of mirror, Niki de Saint Phalle lived for months while the garden was being created. In the presence of the sphinx a riddle-question may arise, "If life is a game of cards we are born without knowing the rules. In spite of this we are all

The Wheel of Fortune *by Jean Tinguely and, in the background, other sculpture/installations*

solitary figures: the *Hermit* and his enigmatic feminine counterpart, the *Oracle*. From the treetops emerges another figure gleaming with mirrors. It is the *Tower of Babel* struck by lightening, symbolized by the sculpture of Jean Tinguely. Just beside the tower is the *Emperor*, the card of male power. It is a complex and fascinating structure, to be visited at leisure. The *Empress* dominates the garden; the enormous sphinx holds within it the *Wagon*, the *Star* and the *Judgement*. Outside is the enchanted area of the chapel of *Temperance* and further on, among the bushes of the Mediterranean *macchia*, the *Moon*.

called upon to play a hand. Are the tarot figures only a game or do they point the way to a philosophy of life?"

Itinerary of visit

For visiting the garden, no particular itinerary is better than any other. We may let ourselves be guided by Niki De Saint Phalle herself who, in her *Garden of the Tarocchi*, led us from the figure of the *Magician* to that of the *Papess* and then on to the fountain of the *Wheel of Fortune*, created by the French artist Jean Tinguely, her companion in art and in life.

Along the border of the pool we come upon *Force*, represented by a delicate girl dominating a dragon. Passing under the arch of the bird of *Sun* we find in sequence *Death, Devil* and the *World*. After having seen the *Madman* and the *Pope* we walk around the *Hanged Man*, in his colorful house filled with mirrors. On the white ceramic tiling can be seen drawings and sketches for the *Wheel of Fortune* and the *Sun*. In the center of a clearing is *Justice*, with his prisoner.

At the edge of the woods the figures of the *Sweethearts* symbolize *Choice*, while from the *macchia* emerge two

To know more

VV. AA., *Niki de Saint Phalle. Il giardino dei Tarocchi*, catalogue of the exhibition, Orbetello Polveriera Guzman 1997, Milan 1997.

Niki de Saint Phalle, *Il giardino dei Tarocchi*, Berna 1997.

Web: www.nikidesaintphalle.com

"The garden of the Tarocchi is not just my garden, it belongs to all those who have helped me to complete it. I am the architect of this garden. I have imposed my vision because I could not do otherwise. This garden has been created with difficulty, with wild enthusiasm, with obsession and more than anything else, with faith. Nothing and no one could have stopped me. As in all fables, along the path that leads to the hidden treasure I have encountered dragons, witches, magicians and the Angel of Temperance".

Niki de Saint Phalle

The garden of Daniel Spoerri
The play of affinities

itinerary, marked by works of art, winds around the villa and through the broad meadow in front of the woods without any precise theme, but following creations brought together by a common intention.

The garden contains 87 works by 42 artists including, in addition to Spoerri himself, Eva Aeppli, Roberto

HOW TO ARRIVE

Take S.S. 2 Cassia headed toward Rome and turn off after Castiglion d'Orcia.
Owner: Fondazione Il Giardino
Address: Loc. Giardino, Seggiano, Grosseto
tel.: +39 0564 950805
E-mail: ilgiardino@ilsilene.it
Visiting hours: from July 1 to Sept. 15, every day from 11:00 am to 8:00 pm; from Sept. 15 to Oct. 31, Tue.-Sun. from 11:00 am to 7:00 pm; from Easter to July 1 Tue.-Sun. from 11:00 am to 8:00 pm; Nov. - March by appointment only
Admission: 10,00 €, reduced 8 € (children students)
Free admission for under 8
Guided visits by reservation 100,00 €
Accessible to the disabled
Restrooms
Café - Bookshop

The Warriors of the Night by Daniel Spoerri

Paradiso, that is, garden, was the name of the place up to two hundred years ago, and the beauty of this garden stretched out over the splendid hillside facing the town of Seggiano is truly heavenly. A fine avenue of ancient plane trees leads to the villa and already in the parking lot the visitor is surrounded by the works of Daniel Spoerri and other artists. The most significant characteristic of this garden of art is to be found in the elective affinities that have linked the Swiss artist to other artists spiritually akin to him. The

Barni, and Roland Topor. The purchase of a large estate gave Spoerri the chance for an intense confrontation with the nature of the place. From this came the idea of displaying works of art outdoors, distributing them along an itinerary similar to that of the sacred woods of Bomarzo, near Viterbo.

The garden, which became a Foundation in 1997, has been the site of exhibitions since 1998, when the first show was held, entitled *The Friends of Daniel Spoerri's Garden.*

From the entrance we proceed toward the great meadow where some of Spoerri's works can be seen: **The Warriors of the Night**, the *Labyrinthine Walled Path,* and the *Grass Divan*. From here the path leads on to the most panoramic point, overlooking the town of Seggiano, where we find another work by Spoerri, **Unicorns/The Navel of the World**. Continuing along the ring walk, we find one of the most significant works in the collection, *Chambre No 13 de l'Hotel Carcassonne Paris 1959-1965,* a representation in bronze of the room in which Spoerri worked during the years indicated in the title. Today a thorough visit can last three hours.

To know more
Il Giardino di Daniel Spoerri,
edited by A. Mazzanti, Florence 1998-99.

Web: www.danielspoerri.org

Eva Aeppli,
Les Faiblesses humaines
(1993-1994)

Daniel Spoerri,
Unicorni-Omphalos,
ombelico del mondo
(1991)

Ester Seidel,
The seer
(1996-1997)

Parco della Sterpaia
An art itinerary through the woods

HOW TO ARRIVE

Between Piombino and Follonica, exiting from S.S. I Aurelia.
Address: Loc. Carlappiano, Piombino, Livorno.
tel.: +39 0565 226445,
E-mail:
prenotazioni@parchivaldicornia.it
Visiting hours: by appointment only for groups and schools
Admission: 4,00 € (one person for schools from April 1 to Sept. 15), reduced 3,00 € (other seasons)
60,00 € in total for groups
The visit lasts two hours
Accessible to the disabled
Restrooms

The book-tree

The itinerary of the monumental forest of Sterpaia represents one of the most recent initiatives in Tuscany to combine elements of naturalist interest with an art itinerary.

This woods, a rare survival of what was once the typical coastal humid forest of the Maremma, is considered a true living monument for its centuries-old oaks, maples and elm trees.

Due to its unique characteristics and the beauty of the place, the forest has been declared a real natural oasis to be preserved intact. It has recently been decided to fence off the area, covering about 24 hectares, to ensure adequate protection for a very fragile ecosystem.

The forest is sheltered by a broad stretch of coastal sand dunes, around which grow clumps of lentiscus, myrtle and juniper bushes, where the presence of the sea can always be felt.

In setting up the itinerary according to the project of Mariachiara Pozzana and opening it to the public, the attempt has been made to emphasize the mystery and sacred nature of this place.

Only through art and poetry is it possible to approach such a natural environment without risk of harming it. In the vicinity of the oak trees most significant for size and shape (the oldest ones have diameters of several meters around the trunk) **works in bronze** by the sculptor Marcello Guasti have been placed. Each sculpture is accompanied by the verses of poets (among them Eugenio Montale, Mario Luzi, Dylan

*Guide map
to the park*

*A work in bronze
by Marcello Guasti*

Thomas and Dino Campana). These poetic signposts meld art with nature, confronting hikers through the woods with the expression of an artist and that of the forest and the trees in their most natural state.

In the vicinity of the park is an educational workshop designed to provide school children with an approach to the marvels of nature and the forest, and a 'book tree' dedicated to the oak.

At the entrance is the '**book tree**'. It consists of a stump with great wooden 'pages' carved by the sculptor Guasti with portraits of the oaks, bearing solemn witnesses to the sacred nature of the woods. It is a tree that summarizes the mythological references to trees as living beings, communicating and teaching.

To know more

Web: www.parchivaldicornia.it

Villa Cetinale
A mingling of sacred and profane

HOW TO ARRIVE

In the vicinity of Sovicille,
south of Siena, take the Siena Porta
San Marco exit from the Firenze-
Siena superstrada (motorway)
Owner: The Lambton family
Address:
Loc. Cetinale, Sovicille, Siena
tel.: +39 0577 311147
fax: +39 0577 311092
E-mail: info@villacetinale.com
villacetinale@gmail.com
Visiting hours: Monday-Friday, 9:30
am - 12:30 pm, by appointment only
Admission: 10,00 €
Accessible to the disabled
Restrooms

The villa

The countryside south of Siena, abounding in sites of rare beauty, arouses emotions that prepare the visitor for Cetinale. Within the park is a splendid formal garden, a number of flower gardens with magnificent roses, peonies, perennials and bulbous plants and above all a splendid Baroque layout with the scope of a landscape sweeping from plain to hillside.

The villa was built by Cardinal Flavio Chigi, a member of the wealthy, powerful family of Sienese bankers who had moved to Rome at the service of the Pope. The building initiative, which lasted from 1676 to 1716, was commissioned of the architect Carlo Fontana, a pupil of Bernini, who had already worked on other projects for the Chigi family (in Rome and San Quirico d'Orcia). The building having been rapidly completed, Cardinal Chigi occupied himself with the exterior layout, which was probably also commissioned of

Fontana. The architect designed a great axis that starts on the plain with the statue of *Hercules*, traverses the villa with its surrounding gardens and arrives as far as the hillside to conclude in a *romitorio*. An itinerary through the sacred and the profane is rendered even more complex by the presence of a 'thebaide' in the surrounding oak woods.

The woods of the 'thebaide' (the name alludes to the desert in Upper Egypt to which, in the 3rd century AD, many Christian hermits fled to lead an ascetic life) grows around a long network of paths and avenues, with statues of saints and hermits thought to be the work of the sculptor Giuseppe Mazzuoli. The woods also holds one of the seven votive chapels dedicated to the sorrows of the Virgin, arranged in a sort of circle embracing Cetinale. It is said that the consecrated *boschetto* was desired by Cardinal Chigi as a place dedicated to the expiation of a particular sin of his, having to do with the death of a rival in love. For some years in the late 17th and early 18th centuries the fa-

The side garden

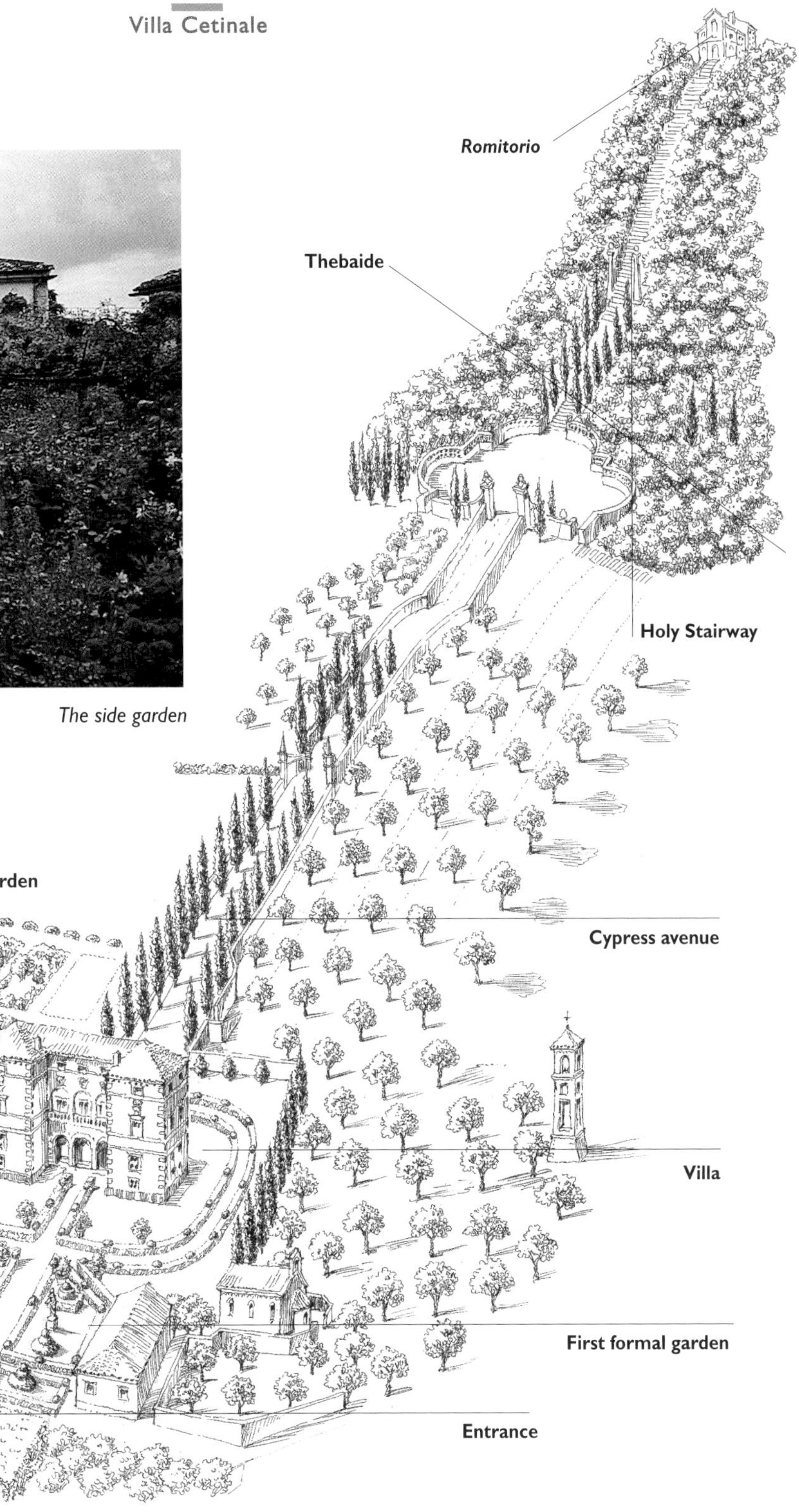

Romitorio

Thebaide

Holy Stairway

Side garden

Cypress avenue

Villa

First formal garden

Entrance

Entrance to the cypress avenue   *The cypress avenue*

mous horserace known as the Palio of Siena was run in these woods. It may be that the figures hewn in stone and scattered through the underbrush, such as the *Tortoise* and the *Snail* (attributed by some to Mazzuoli), allude expressly to the Palio.

On the hill facing the villa is the *romitorio*. A long avenue now partially lined by cypresses starts from the villa and runs through a monumental terra-cotta portal decorated by busts and statues in classical style. It then continues up to a vast open space at the foot of the hill. We now find ourselves in a theatrical space where the designer has staged a religious scene; it is obvious that the *romitorio* serves the function of theatrical backdrop. On the facade of the building, several stories high, is a great cross. The *romitorio* is reached by climbing a steep stairway of nearly 200 steps, immersed in the green woods that surrounds it. Up until the last few years of the 19th century this place was inhabited by 12 hermit friars who visited the chapel in the woods once a month.

Itinerary of visit

From the gate on the southern side of the property appears in the distance, at the end of a long tree-lined

about two hundred meters to the open area at the foot of the Holy Stairway. From here there is a steep climb up the steps to the *romitorio*, from which we can admire the garden, the villa and a landscape still miraculously preserved. From the *romitorio* we descend along the path on the right to the 'thebaide', where numerous paths running through it, marked with statues, invite the visitor. From here we return to the exit.

To know more

O. Guaita, *Le ville della Toscana*, Rome 1997.

S. Bajard, *Villas et jardins de Toscane*, Paris 1992.

H. Acton, *Tuscan Villas*, London 1973.

Web: www.villacetinale.com

avenue, the statue of *Hercules*. Through this gate we enter the formal garden with hedges of box and topiaries, embellished by potted citruses and seasonal flowers. The back of the villa and the chapel face on the garden.

On the left a **group of gardens flowers** in splendor, a real paradise for garden lovers. From beyond the villa the composition can be observed as a whole.

A broad **avenue of cypresses** slopes gently upward to the small buildings that mark the **entrance**. Here the avenue narrows to continue, now treeless, for

In this page: two views of the side garden

Chronology

15th c. Cetinale is owned by the rich and powerful Chigi family, Sienese bankers who then move to Rome at the service of the Pope.
1676 The work of transforming the farm of Cetinale into a manorial residence begins with the building of the villa.
1676-1678 The formal garden and the annexes to the villa are built.
After 1680 Numerous sculptures, probably inspired by subjects of classical culture, are placed around the villa, along the avenue and in the piazzale. Many of the sculptures, the work of Giuseppe Mazzuoli, have now been lost or moved elsewhere.
1687 The colossal statue of Hercules is finished.
1698-1705 The great oak woods stretching to the east of the villa is transformed into the 'thebaide'.
1716 The *romitorio* is built.
1977 The Chigi family sell Cetinale to Lord Anthony Lambton. Today it is owned by his children subsequent to Lord Lambton's death in 2006.

Villa di Vicobello
A masterpiece by Baldassarre Peruzzi

HOW TO ARRIVE

In the city of Siena.
Owner: Selina Bonelli Zondadari
Address: Viale Bianchi Bandinelli 14, Siena
tel e fax: +39 0577 332460
e-mail: gardentour@vicobello.it
Visits by appointment only
Admission: 15,00 €
Possibility of light lunch for groups of 10 or more
Partially accessible to the disabled
Restrooms

The lemon garden

aia, on the southeast by the lemon garden and on the northwest by the *boschetto* of ilexes.

The heraldic emblem of the Chigi family, the mountain, recurs in the great boxwood topiaries from

Both villa and garden were built by the Chigi family in the 16th century. The project is generally attributed to Baldassarre Peruzzi, the architect of many villas and gardens in the territory of Siena. The building, which exists in close symbiosis with the surrounding garden, is undoubtedly one of the masterpieces of villa architecture in the Sienese territory. In 1770 Giacomo Casanova stayed here, as guest of Violante Chigi, who became a close friend of the writer and philosopher at the death of her husband. According to the scheme customary in Tuscany, the garden was terraced in front of the building. The 16th century design conferred perfect spatial organization on the villa, inserting it at the center of a courtyard which was bounded on the back by the the service annexes and the *limon-*

modern times and appears again in the forecourt of the villa and on the third terrace.

The spatial scheme is organized along two main axes, one at right angles to the villa, the other parallel to it, cutting the lemon garden in half. To this simple, austere plan was added, in the 19th century, a third garden below the second terrace, which now houses the orchid greenhouse. In the forecourt of the villa stands the **chapel**, a building of very elegant lines.

Itinerary of visit

From the courtyard behind the villa we enter the **lemon garden** through an elegant terra-cotta portal. The garden is bounded by walls lined with hedges of evergreen and, on the northern side, the

The chapel beside the villa

The garden of fruit trees

limonaia where citrus trees were sheltered in winter. It is divided into four compartments, each in turn divided into four sectors with a circular element at the center. Based on the perfect symmetry, balance and the rationality of the parts, it may be presumed that the garden's design dates from the 16th century. This refined geometry is emphasized by the hedges of box that border the lawns dotted with lemon urns. At the back of the eastern wall and along the entrance axis a terra-cotta exedra closes off the garden, enhancing the intimate, enclosed effect. The exedra, attributable for the simple elegance of its design to Baldassarre Peruzzi, is composed of an ample niche surmounted by a molded pediment bearing at its center the Chigi coat of arms. Within it is a circular stone bench and a table.

A ramp of stairs connects the lemon garden to the **orchard**, where fruit trees were probably grown originally (according to the Tuscan tradition in which the terrace below the house was usually designated as *pomario*, or orchard).

Divided into three sections, each in turn subdivided into four beds bordered in box, it is embellished by the splendid flowering of antique roses of 19th century taste. Below the ancient fruit garden a narrow terrace with an orchid greenhouse called the 'botanical garden' concludes the eastern side of the garden.

The last terrace is that of the belvedere, reached by descending a double ramp of stairs. This part of the garden ends in an unusual fishpond in the shape of a half moon.

To know more

VV.AA., *Vita in villa nel senese*, edited by L. Bonelli Conenna and E. Pacini, Ospedaletto/Pisa 2000.

Web: www.vicobello.it

Castello di Celsa
"Tornati a Celsa, e guarda Che la quiete mia non ti sia tolta"

HOW TO ARRIVE

In the vicinity of Sovicille, south of Siena, take the Siena Porta San Marco exit from the Firenze - Siena superstrada (motorway).
Owner: Livia Aldobrandini Pediconi
Address: Celsa, Sovicille, Siena
tel.: + 39 06 6861138
fax: +39 06 68195912
e-mail: info@castellodicelsa.com
Visiting hours: only upon presentation of request in writing and for groups of at least 4 persons
Admission: 8,00 €
Restrooms

sang the Sienese poet and humanist, "tornati a Celsa, e guarda/che la quiete mia non ti sia tolta" (You my little song /rough and unrefined / come back to Celsa and watch / that my peace is never stolen from you). In the ancient woods and the garden with its adjacent hunting park, silence is still today the fundamental element. The only sounds to be heard are those of wind, water and birds. This absence of sound becomes

The fishpond

Situated on the crest of a hill overlooking the Rosia valley, the castle takes its name from the Sienese family Celsi who built in near the end of the 13th century. In the 16th century it was transformed into a villa, probably by Mino Celsi, a man of letters and member of the Sienese *Accademia degli Intronati*, who owned it together with his uncle Cristofano. Celsi recalls the shady peace of the estate at the beginning of his translation of Horace's second Ode, in a dedication to the Archbishop of Siena Francesco Bandini Piccolomini. "Tu canzonetta mia rozza/ed incolta",

music, melding with the broad expanse of the great terraced lawns, cultivated in the past, that follow each other in succession to merge into the surrounding landscape. In the distance appears a view of Siena, perfect and reassuring as in a 15th century painting.
The name of the castle is linked to the work of Baldassarre Peruzzi (1481-1537), the architect of numerous Sienese villas and gardens. He was responsible for the circular chapel built of brick, elegant in style, and probably also for the terraced wall parallel to the entrance avenue and the **terraced garden** sloping down the hill

The castle seen from the garden

toward the valley, with its travertine stone vases and potted citrus trees.

With these transformations, in keeping with the Renaissance concept of villa, the Medieval castle found itself inserted in a logic of perspective and symmetry. The new wing formed an inner courtyard closed off by a wall with three elegant portals opening onto the surrounding landscape (a solution similar to the one adopted in the castle of Belcaro).

The gardens of Celsa, transformed during the Baroque period, consist today of the 16th century terraced garden and the side garden with its fine hedge of cypresses, great **fishpond** and parapet decorated in relief patterns.

In the late 19th and early 20th century Maria Antinori Aldobrandini decided to renovate the castle in neo-Gothic style, commissioning the architect Mariani to carry out this project.

Luminous mullioned windows in the facade as well as imitation crenellations and battlements were added. Presumably during the same period numerous tall trees, mainly cedars and ornamental conifers, were planted. Today these trees stand out on the great lawn in front of the fishpond.

In the postwar years Luisa Aldobrandini, mother of the present owner, made another change.

The garden in front of the building was embellished by box beds planted in the shape of the Aldobrandini coat of arms, composed of stars and rakes, and the cypress hedge that links the garden to the fishpond at the edge of the hunting park was added.

A cypress topiary

The avenue leading to the fishpond

*The garden with box beds
and the semicircular pool*

stone, water and evergreens

"The Italian garden does not exist for its flowers; its flowers exist for it: they are a late and infrequent adjunct to its beauties, a parenthetical grace counting only as one more touch in the general effect of enchantment. This is no doubt partly explained by the difficulty of cultivating any but spring flowers in so hot and dry a climate, and the result has been a wonderful development of the more permanent effects to be obtained from the three other factors in garden-composition – marble, water and perennial verdure – and the achievement, by their skilful blending, of a charm independent of the seasons.
It is hard to explain to the modern garden-lover, whose whole conception of the charm of gardens is formed of successive pictures of flower-loveliness, how this effect of enchantment can be produced by anything so dull and monotonous as a mere combination of clipped green and stone-work".

E. Wharton, *Italian Villas and their Gardens*, New York 1904

Itinerary of visit

The imposing castle dominates the terraced plain stretching before it. The entrance avenue, flanked by rural buildings, some of which are used today for country tourism, leads directly to the castle. A splendid tier of *terra-cotta* and travertine steps radiating outward leads to the first level and then to the courtyard. From there we descend to the **enclosed garden**, adorned with fine statues, fountains in the wall and a **semicircular pool**. At the sides stand two buildings; the one on the left used as *limonaia* is lit up in spring by the flowering of 'Alba Plena' Banksian roses. Returning to the castle we continue eastward along the **avenue** flanked by clipped hedges of cypress. Through well-kept lawns the path leads to the splendid **fish-pond**. Of semicircular shape, it has a wall decorated with river gods, marine animals and travertine urns.

From here a system of straight paths radiates out through the great park of ilexes, once used for hunting.

To know more

Web: www.castellodicelsa.com

Geggiano
A theater in a garden

HOW TO ARRIVE

In the vicinity of Geggiano,
along S.S. 408.
Owner: the Boscu Bianchi
Bandinelli family
Address: Via di Geggiano 1,
Pianella, Siena
tel.: + 39 0577 356879
e-mail: info@villadigeggiano.com
Visiting hours: by appointment only.
Guided visits for groups
of at least 8 persons
Luncheons, dinners, wine and olive
oil tasting (own production)
organized upon request
Olive oil and wine sold
Visitors are greeted directly
by the owners
Bookshop

*This page:
the orchard*

*Next page:
the villa seen
from the orchard*

*At right:
the theater*

The estate of Geggiano, crowning a low hill, is reached through a long *cerchiata* of ancient ilexes. The villa was created by reconstructing an older building. In the 1760s, when Domenico Bianchi Bandinelli married his second wife Cecilia Chigi Zondadari, it is probable that a modest manor house with tower was transformed into a beautiful country residence (the tower can still be seen at the center of the building).

On the occasion of this work, the fine garden still admired today was also created. The part of the garden in front of the villa, familiarly known as the *piazzone*, on the same axis as the building, is closed off at the back by an interesting **'garden theater'**. It is reached by a central path that, running between parterres of box, connects the building to the garden architecture.

An axis at right angles to the one that links the villa to the little theater leads to the *selvatico* on one side and to the **orchard/garden** on the other, distinguished by an elegant semicircular fishpond.

An encircling wall decorated with terra-cotta sculptures surrounds the entire orchard and garden, opening to the outside through six monumental gates, they too decorated with terra-cotta sculptures.

The 'garden theater' is a typical feature of the 17th century Baroque garden. Created at a relatively late date, Geggiano's garden theater is nonetheless the finest element in the entire composition. We know for certain that it was constructed before 1783, the year in

which Vittorio Alfieri recited one of his tragedies there (the chamber in which the poet slept, furnished with the opulent bed with baldachin of the times, can still be seen. The cultural interests of the Bianchi Bandinelli family are clear; in addition to inviting such a famous poet as Alfieri, they also called upon foreign artists to work in the villa).

In front of the garden theater stage stand two brick buildings bearing the coats of arms of the Bianchi Bandinelli and Chigi Zondadari families on the coping. Niches in these buildings hold statues of *Comedy* and *Tragedy*. A tall cypress tree heightens the perspective effect, making the stage seem deeper than it really is.

To know more

L. Bonelli Conenna and E. Pacini, *Vita in villa nel Senese*, Ospedaletto/Pisa, 2000.

Web: www.villadigeggiano.com

Chronology

Before 1530 The Geggiano estate, a simple country residence probably surrounded by an orchard/garden, belongs to the De Santi family.

1530 Geggiano, brought as dowry, becomes one of the possessions of the noble Sienese family Bianchi Bandinelli.

c. 1768 The country residence is transformed into a true villa and is furnished with an interesting garden centering around the 'garden theater'.

End of 18th c. The villa is splendidly frescoed by the Tyrolean painter Ignazio Molder, who in the long gallery on the ground floor, depicts various aspects of country life, the cycles of nature and scenes inspired by the Commedia dell'Arte. In this work Molder draws inspiration from the drawings of Giuseppe Zocchi and the engravings of Francesco Bartolozzi. The pictorial program is further enriched by portraits of famous personages of the times: from the lord and lady of the house Anton Domenico and Cecilia to the famous singer and musician Perellino, shown with his actress daughters. Nature and theater are linked in a single representation.

1824 Ownership passes from Giulio Ranuccio Bianchi Bandinelli, first Napoleonic prefect of the Department of the Ombrone and then Governor of Siena, to his eldest son Mario, who makes no great changes. From Mario, through variousch ereditary transitions, it comes down to its present owners.

L'Apparita
The Sienese landscape becomes a garden

The entrance to the villa

HOW TO ARRIVE

In the vicinity of Ginestreto,
along S.S. 223.
Owner: Paolo Guiso
Address: Strada Ginestreto 1, Siena
tel.: +39 0577 394241
fax: + 39 0577 394241
Visiting hours: by appointment only
(to be booked a month in advance)
Partially accessible to the disabled
Restrooms

Situated to the south of Siena, in a dominating, panoramic position, the fine brick building with its splendid side loggia is traditionally attributed to Baldassarre Peruzzi.

Even in the absence of archival documents to confirm it, the villa, so elegant and harmonious, truly seems to indicate the hand of a master. It is not really a villa but a manor house, that is a fine, comfortable dwelling place but not one so elegant as to be surrounded by a sumptuous garden. Before 1966 the garden did not exist; only the Sienese countryside extended all around the building.

The garden was created by Pietro Porcinai for the present owner, who was prepared to understand and strongly support the proposals of the great landscape artist, undoubtedly highly innovative. The garden of the Apparita is one of Porcinai's most original creations. It reiterates, in fact, the salient characteristics of the Tuscan landscape, transforming them into a garden.

This conceptual procedure has led to the invention of what can be called a garden/landscape, an absolute, emblematic place where the Tuscan landscape is reproduced in synthesis, and where Porcinai may have reached his highest peak of creativity.

Although today the initiative seems minimalist, so natural and harmonious is the result, Porcinai has in reality wrought profound changes.

The transformations brought about by the architect can be clearly evaluated only by examining aerial photographs taken before, in which the agricultural nature of the area is clear.

By large-scale earth movement the landscape artist reinterpreted the entire system of access roads, now moved lower and further away from the house. The avenue rises with great naturalness through olive groves flanked by clumps of Scotch broom, which seem to have existed forever but have instead been artfully planted.

We then arrive at the quadrangular parking lot, lowered so that it is invisible from the house, partially covered by roofing. From here a gently sloping path leads up to the house between two steep banks covered with lavender to form a sort of plant gallery.

The **front door**, rendered monumental by an original arch of ivy, opens in the simple brick facade of the building.

From here the path becomes circular, running around the house to the **garden theater**. Composed of simple benches and surrounded by hedges of broom, the essential structure of the theater recalls, for its situation, Greek theaters, which always faced on a panorama so beautiful as to evoke a sense of the divine. Few but fine terra-cotta ornaments and some **inscriptions** are the elements by which the eye is caught before sweeping over the landscape in the direction of Siena.

The Apparita garden is essential and evocative as only a perfect Sienese landscape can be. Gentle rolling hills modulate a horizon rhythmically broken by the vertical soaring of cypresses against the sky.

The Tuscan landscape takes on the appearance of an ideogram, calling to mind a page of Japanese signs. Framed by two cypresses, Siena appears in the distance, like a Renaissance model of the ideal city, its profile barely softened by the summer haze.

One of the inscriptions in the garden

The theater

The benches in the theater

Horti Leonini
Eternal springtime

HOW TO ARRIVE

Along S.S. 2 Cassia headed
toward Rome.
Address: Piazza della Libertà,
San Quirico d'Orcia
tel.: +39 0577 897211 (Municipality of
S. Quirico d'Orcia, Tourism Bureau)
Visiting hours: from 8:00 am to sunset
(seasonal variations);
possible visits in the evening
in summer only
Free admission
Guided visits by appointment

A round 1560, Grand Duke Cosimo I granted to Diomede Leoni owner-ship of the area, situated under the towns wall of San Quirico d'Orcia.
The construction of the garden went on for years and in 1581 it was not yet complete, although Leoni had, it seems, already spent large amounts in renovating the **town wall** standing along one side of the garden.

The owner was authorized to build a path on top of the wall so that both the garden and the valley of the Orcia could be admired from above.

The garden was called *Horti Leonini* from the name of its owner and creator, and the lion appears in fact on the two heads placed on the entrance portal.

Originally there were four entrances, the main one on the city square, the one in the back near the Church of Santa Maria ad Hortos, the one situated halfway

down the northern wall, marked by two pilasters, and the little door above, opened in the wall.

Through a vestibule paved in brick and enclosed by walls and clipped ilexes, we enter a ***parterre*** in the shape of an elongated rhombus. The design of the

The parterre *near the town walls*

parterre is highly original: a star-shaped pattern of tri-angular beds visually enlarges the space available, which is animated still further by the different heights of the box hedges around the beds.

At the center stands a statue of Cosimo III, sculpted in 1688 by Giuseppe Mazzuoli and coming from Palaz-zo Chigi in San Quirico. Through a ramp cut out of the *selvatico* of ilex trees the central avenue leads to the upper level, where a great lawn stretches as far as the town walls.

On this lawn, bounded by a majestic 'crown' of ilexes, once stood the imposing Medieval tower, destroyed by German troops in 1944. From here another ramp

The parterre

leads down to an avenue of ilexes trimmed to form a wall of vegetation, and then to the rose garden (recently restructured) that bounds the lower part of the garden.

We know that Diomede Leoni had a house in the garden, and that he was granted permission to cut four windows and a little door in the town wall. The house may be identified as the *palazzina* leaning against the wall on the southwest side. Inside it a fireplace bears the inscription *"nec procul nec longe"* ("neither far away nor for long"), clearly expressing the love of its former owner for his garden and his wish never to leave this place for long.

The garden is filled with inscriptions recalling themes dear to Diomede, as demonstration of the profound meaning it must have held for the man who created it and lived in it: *"omitte mirari beatae / fumum et opes strepitumq. Romae"* (Be no longer fascinated by the frenetic activity of happy Rome"); *"peregrino labore fessi / venimus larem ad nostrum"* (wearied by the fatigue of wandering we have returned to our hearth"); *"nihil agis / insidias in me componis inanes"* ("be calm. Sooth my futile worries"); *"hic vitabis aestus"* ("here you will find shelter from the torrid heat"); *"hic ver assiduum"* ("here is eternal springtime").

Giardino di Palazzo Piccolomini
A window on the Val d'Orcia

The garden seen from the palazzo

HOW TO ARRIVE

Along S.S. 2 Cassia in the direction of Rome.
The palace is in the center of Pienza, about 50 km from Siena.
The garden can be visited only on the occasion of very special events but may be seen from the museum inside the palace
Call center: +39 0577 286300

This little garden, whose surface area is about the same area as that of the palazzo, admirably exemplifies the type of walled garden that, in the 15th century, represented the worthy completion of a palace in the city. In the 15th century, an open, panoramic space on an axis with the courtyard was a truly innovative concept. Enea Silvio Piccolomini (who became Pope Pius II in 1457) commissioned Bernardo Rossellino to transform the little town of Corsignano into a modern city, which was given the name Pienza. The work went on from 1459 to 1464, the year when both the client and the architect died. In his *Commentari* Pope Pius II describes the construction of the garden, conceived as a garden and "hanging orchard, suitable for grapevines and other trees". The land was filled in and leveled to have a flat plane in front of the house. Planted to fruit trees, the place was furnished with a stone balustrade and seats "brightened with colored pinnacles that form a gallant spectacle from afar". The garden appears today in the layout given it in 1910, on the occasion of the restoration of the palazzo built by Silvio Piccolomini and carried out on the basis of documentary sources, with the intention of harmoniously reconstructing the original scheme. Divided into four sections bordered by **double hedges of box**, the garden has a central fountain, rounded topiaries of laurel, gravel paths and beds of flowering roses. It is enclosed by an ivy-covered wall; on the southern side three windows have been opened in place of the original parapet, presumably damaged during the years of neglect. The simultaneous view of the palace courtyard and the garden, in the blinding light of the Sienese sky, is an unforgettable experience. Looking into the garden through the openings in the wall we remain suspended in a timeless space enveloping the landscape of the Val d'Orcia.

To know more

M. Mangiavacchi, *I giardini del Senese fra '800 e '900: sei esempi a confronto*, in "La memoria, il tempo, la storia nel giardino italiano fra '800 e '900", edited by V. Cazzato, Rome 1999.

Web: www.palazzopiccolominipienza.it

La Foce
A landscape of giants and demigods

HOW TO ARRIVE

Between Chianciano Terme and Pienza, Chianciano Terme exit from the Firenze-Roma A1 highway.
Owner: Benedetta Origo
Address: Strada della Vittoria 61, Chianciano Terme, Siena
tel. and fax: +39 0578 69101
e-mail: info@lafoce.com
Visiting hours: only on Wednesday afternoon. Guided visits only from November to March at 3:00 pm and 4:00 pm; from April to October at 3:00 pm, 4:00 pm, 5:00 pm and 6:00 pm; from the last Saturday of March to the last Saturday of October every hour 10:00 am - 12:00 pm, 3:00 - 6:00 pm.
Admission: 10,00 €
Partially accessible to the disabled
Restrooms

The geometric garden

In the extraordinary landscape of the Val d'Orcia, arid and almost barren in summer, slashed by the deep eroded ditches of the *crete*, Villa La Foce and its splendid garden are an unexpected oasis of serene repose. This is undoubtedly one of the most beautiful modern gardens in Tuscany. It is probable that the owner Iris Origo, a refined writer and author of the historical novel "The Merchant of Prato", perceived this place as a landscape marked by striking contrasts. In the late 1920s she and her husband Antonio bought an abandoned estate and transformed it into a magnificent villa with a model farm. The English architect and landscape artist Cecil Pinsent, a friend of Iris Origo, was commissioned to carry out the work, in a project that went on until 1939. He created the great garden in different stages, but always according to a unitary logic, drawing inspiration from the formal gardens of classic Italian tradition. Pinsent also renovated the building and designed the *limonaia* and other annexes.

In 1927 the first formal garden, bounded to the south by a wall with a fountain and a green grotto concealed by a dome of laurel, was built in front of the house. From here a path leads to the **lemon garden**, begun in 1933. It is adorned by box trimmed in spherical shapes and bordered along the sides by herbaceous plants and splendid peonies. The transverse axis of the garden continues, rising along an avenue of cypress trees to the top of the hill.

In 1939 the monumental **geometric garden** was laid out below the lemon garden. It is reached by descending a stairway built of Rapolano travertine. Below the stairway is a grotto. Bordered by great box hedges, dominated by four magnolias and enclosed by high walls of cypresses, the triangular space ends in a pool and a statuary group.

A long pergola of wisteria bounds the formal garden at the top, while on the other side of the *berceau* runs a narrow terrace containing a rose garden with borders of lavender and herbaceous perennials, among which emerge clumps of *aubretia* and *alyssum*. Following the wisteria pergola we arrive at a strikingly panoramic spot overlooking the broad **landscape** of the Val d'Orcia, marked by the avenue of cypresses planted by Iris Origo in homage to Florentine 15th century painting.

Continuing up the slope we find an informal garden with aromatic and Mediterranean plants where the geometric structure of the garden gradually drifts off into the woods.

Near the woods is a little family graveyard, where Iris' son, who died at the age of six, is buried. This space too was designed by Pinsent as a garden enclosed by cypresses with tombs placed amid box beds and a chapel in Renaissance style.

To know more

Web: www.lafoce.com

The formal garden

Cecil Pinsent
the architect of gardens

Cecil Ross Pinsent was one of the most important garden architects in Tuscany in the first half of the 20th century. Born in Uruguay in 1884, he returned with his family to England while still a child. There he studied architecture at the Architectural Association of London. In 1906 he moved to Florence, where he met Bernard Berenson, the famous art historian who was one of his first clients. In 1909 Pinsent worked, in fact, on Villa I Tatti, at Ponte a Mensola near Settignano. The results of this project were brilliant, and numerous others followed, with the architect creating the gardens of Villa Le Balze (1911), Villa Medici (1915), and Villa La Foce (starting in 1927), his longest and most ardently enthusiastic project.

Pinsent's gardens revive the architectural nature of the Italian formal garden, through the use of box hedges and topiaries long with grottoes, fountains and statues that the architect himself designed with great creative talent and craftsmanship, frequently carrying out the material execution as well. Better than any other architect, he knew how to interpret the desires of his clients, for the most part British or Americans members of the highly cultivated, sophisticated colony enamored of Florence and Tuscany.

"Below me lay the fields beside the river – land potentially fertile, but then fallow, which would be flooded when the rains came by the encroaching river-bed. Against the sky, behind the black rocks of Radicofani, dark clouds were gathering for a storm [...] Suddenly an overwhelming wave of longing came over me for the gentle, trim Florentine landscape of my childhood or for green English fields and big trees – and most of all, for a pretty house and garden to come home to in the evening. I felt the landscape around me to be alien, inhuman – built on a scale fit for demi-gods and giants, but not for us".

I. Origo, *Images and shadows*, London, 1970

The geometric garden

La Ragnaia di San Giovanni d'Asso
If not here, where?

At right:
the wood of the Ragnaia with
Sheppard Craige's works

Next page:
the lower part
of the wood

HOW TO ARRIVE

Take Autostrada A1 Firenze-Roma,
exit at Valdichiana, direction Sinalunga,
and continue toward S. Giovanni
d'Asso.
Address: Provincial Road del Pecorile,
San Giovanni d'Asso, Siena
e-mail: info@laragnaia.com
Private park open to the public
Free entrance every day from
dawn to sunset.
Children under 12 must be
accompanied
No camping, no smoking permitted

At San Giovanni d'Asso, the relic of an ancient *ragnaia* transformed by nature and the years into a shady grove of ilexes served as inspiration for the American artist Sheppard Craige, who with his wife has converted this steep, solitary place into a garden open to all visitors.

Sheppard Craige likes to recall the motto *Se non qui, dove?* (If not here, where?). At a remote, unspecified time in history, when the forest was governed by wise men, this motto referred to the grove and its force of attraction; it soon came to represent the link between the *ragnaia* and the place.

The term *ragnaia* means a grove of trees where, since the Middle Ages, in the gardens of the Mediterranean basin, birds were caught with nets, called *ragne* or *ragnatele*. In the Tuscan countryside, the place name *ragnaia* is surprisingly frequent, for the reason that every self-respecting garden or agricultural estate had to include a *ragnaia*, used for hunting but also for resting in the cool shade of the trees in summer. The *ragnaia* was almost always planted to yew trees, their foliage clipped to form a great hedge, with a few pine trees waving their branches above to call the birds that would adorn the prince's table. Planted along the sides of the great hedges were lentisc, myrtle and other shrubs producing abundant berries, the birds' favourite food, in autumn.

A long green corridor leads to a series of 'garden rooms' where mineral elements, kerbs, stone slabs and plinths converse with nature under the sign of the purest Renaissance tradition, but in continuous evolution. These 'rooms', connecting with one another, lead down a staircase to the **lower part of the ragnaia**. But before descending, pause to admire the sweeping view over the central part of the garden, where the artist's work can be seen at a glance.

With a group of stone and brick constructions he has created an environment where the natural and the artificial blend organically into the connective tissue of poetry, consisting of numerous inscriptions inviting visitors to pause, reflect and interpret. The play of free interpretation enchants the visitor as he passes from the *Altar of Scepticism* to the *Centre of the Universe*, and on to the *Oracle of Thyself*.

The **Wood** created by Sheppard Craige is not designed to offer precise answers, but to evoke a personal, individual response from each visitor. The bronze and terracotta works of the artist Frances Lansing adorn many of these areas.

After having created this forest with the help of numerous young people from San Giovanni d'Asso, Craige reached out of the woods and began to design a new geometric garden, which is now in the process of growing, acquiring an increasingly natural air with the passage of the years.

To know more

S. Craige, *Il bosco della Ragnaia*, Ed. della Ragnaia, 2004
S. Craige, *Words in the Wood*, Ed. della Ragnaia, 2007
Web: www.laragnaia.com

Castello di Brolio
A neo-Medieval garden

HOW TO ARRIVE
Near Castellina in Chianti, Poggibonsi exit from the Firenze-Siena superstrada (motorway).
Owner: Baron Bettino Ricasoli
Address: Brolio, Gaiole in Chianti, Siena
tel.: +39 0577 7301
fax: +39 0577 730225
E-mail: barone@ricasoli.it
Visiting hours: from March to Nov. Mon.-Fri. 10:30 am - 3:00 pm, Sat.-Sun. 10:30 am
(reservation required)
In addition to the castle and park, the wine cellars, vineyards and museum are open to visitors
Restrooms

The garden in front of the castle

The castle, from time immemorial an outpost of great strategic importance in the wars between Florence and Siena, has been destroyed and rebuilt several times over the course of the centuries. The present aspect of the estate is however due almost entirely to the 19th century initiative of Bettino Ricasoli, the Iron Baron whose name is closely linked to the history of the Italian Risorgimento.

Around 1835 Ricasoli decided to rebuild a neo-Gothic castle over the old Medieval ruins. The castle was then completed by the Sienese architect Giuseppe Partini (1842-1895). The vast and complex building was built of brick (typical of Siena, but less common in the Chianti). This makes it quite easy to distinguish the 19th century renovation from the Medieval remains consisting of the ancient encircling wall and the base of the castle keep.

Itinerary of visit

An avenue of cypresses leads up to the castle through the so-called 'English woods' planted by Bettino and Vincenzo Ricasoli starting in the 1840s. The Ricasolis gave a romantic touch to the park, but focused not so much to the design of the whole as on the selection of the species, in keeping with the fashion of the time for botanical collections. At Brolio rare and exotic species were planted, in particular conifers grown from seeds that Bettino and Vincenzo exchanged with other collectors or brought home from their travels: the sequioa (*Sequoia sempervirens*), the Spanish fir (*Abies pinsapo*), the Himalayan cedar (*Cedrus deodara*) and many other species still to be seen today. The park occupies the northern side of the hill (as can be seen from a *cabreo*, or map of the farm dated 1838), arriving to touch on some of the castle buildings.

A small and recent formal garden of simple geomet-

The garden below the castle bastions

ric design lies before the main facade of the castle. Low box hedges border parterres of lavender cotton (*Santolina chamaecyparissus L.*). Nearby stand ancient trees: an ilex (*Quercus ilex L.*) and a great sterculia (*Sterculia sp.*), unfortunately damaged by cannon fire in July 1944.

From the bastions of the wall, which opens to the south over a marvelous panorama of vineyards and woods sweeping from Monte Amiata to Volterra, can be seen a fine **Italian garden**.

Here in the past was the castle moat, probably a 19th century reinterpretation of formal Renaissance models. The garden follows the curve of the wall with a simple, elegant geometric design of box hedges decorated with potted citruses. A long row of Bengali roses separates it from the surrounding countryside.

At the death of Bettino and Vincenzo the park was cared for first by Elisabetta, Bettino's daughter, and then by his grandson Giovanni, both of them ardently botany enthusiasts. Giovanni was a friend of Giuseppe Gaeta, the creator of the Moncioni park near Montevarchi, and author, in 1899, of the *Catalogo delle specie presenti nel parco di Brolio*.

To know more

L. Bosi, *Il Chianti di villa in villa*, Rome 1985.

L. Bosi, *Le ville del Chianti*, Pistoia d.

O. Guaita, *Le ville della Toscana*, Rome 1997.

Web: www.ricasoli.it

Chronology

1009 The first information on Brolio dates from this year. Bonifacio, Marchese of Tuscany, grants the property to the monks of the Badia Fiesolana.

1432 The castle of Brolio is forced to surrender to the attacks of the Sienese militia led by Antonio Petrucci, who holds prisoner for some time members of the Ricasoli family, yielding only to the Florentine troops led by Neri Capponi.

1478 The castle is attacked and almost entirely destroyed by Aragonese troops. It is then rebuilt by the Florentines due to its important strategic position in the Sienese territory.

1530 The castle returns to Florentine jurisdiction after having been again destroyed by Siena during the siege of Florence. Under the Grand Duchy grandiose projects are planned for its restoration and enlargement, which then become useless with the peace stipulated between Florence and Siena. Having lost its strictly military function, the castle becomes the manorial residence and farm of the Ricasoli family.

1835 Bettino Ricasoli decides to restore the castle in Gothic style. The project for the park is drawn up by Bettino Ricasoli himself assisted by his brother Vincenzo, an expert botanist.

1843 Grand Duke Leopolo II orders built the new road that joins Gaiole to Castelnuovo Berardenga. The event is celebrated by stone inscriptions placed on this occasion at the beginning of the new access avenue (flanked by cypress trees) at the desire of Bettino Ricasoli.

21st c. The estate belongs to the Ricasoli family. The area of the English woods has only recently been restored.

Badia a Coltibuono
A Medieval orchard

HOW TO ARRIVE

In the immediate vicinity of Gaiole, Valdarno exit toward Montevarchi from the Firenze-Roma A1 highway.
Owner: the Stucchi-Prinetti family
Address: Badia a Coltibuono, Gaiole in Chianti, Siena
tel.: +39 0577 74481
fax: +39 0577 744839
e-mail: info@coltibuono.com
Visiting hours: May - Oct. always open with visits every hour from 2:00 to 5:00 pm
Admission: 5,00 €
Free admission for children
Guided visits
with wine sampling can be booked

The badia

Badia a Coltibuono is situated on a hilltop not far from the important Etruscan archaeological area of Cetamura, where a long ridge marks the boundary between Chianti and Valdarno, on the road that links Gaiole in Chianti to Montevarchi.

Since the Middle Ages Coltibuono has been the vital center of a great agricultural estate that has grown and flourished over the centuries, also through donations to the Vallombrosian Abbey given by land-owners in the area.

Still today Coltibuono is surrounded by vast conifer woods planted for the first time by the monks who followed San Giovanni Gualberto.

The most striking aspect of the place is the extraor-dinary conservation of the surrounding landscape, which forms a background to the buildings and the **garden** of rare beauty.

The garden, supported by a wall on one of its longer sides, has been replanted in rather recent times and still bears traces of the ancient plots of the Medieval orchard, clearly visible. The vast rectangular space is divided by perpendicular paths into seven sections occupying the lower level of the garden. The paths are partially covered by a rustic **pergola** of grapevines, wisteria and laburnum. At the end, on the edge of the road, stone steps lead down to another small formal garden.

Facing on the largest sector, divided by boxwood hedges, are the windows of the monastery, now a private residence.

At the center is a simple rectangular basin in stone around which winds the complex design of the hedges, bordering beds of roses decorated with topiaries and potted citrus trees. Some of the square sectors are planted to lawn, others to fruit trees.

Among the latter a Medieval orchard has been skillfully reinterpreted in a modern key, reiterating the division into plots containing aromatic and medicinal plants, flowering perennials, peonies and raspberries.

To know more

F. Majnoni, *La Badia a Coltibuono. Storia di una proprietà*, Florence 1981.

Web: www.coltibuono.com

The pergola and the formal garden

The formal garden

Chronology

770 The first core of the Badia is mentioned in a document from the Ricasoli archives.

11th c. Coltibuono passes under the control of the Benedictine Abbey of Vallombrosa.

1446 Paolo da Montemigliaio, the new Abbot of Coltibuono, begins to improve the property.

1488 Giovanni de' Medici, the future Pope Leo X, takes possession of the Abbey.

c. 1710 New major projects for the transformation of the building complex.

1810 Subsequent to the Napoleonic edict that determines suppression of the religious corporations, the monks of Coltibuono are forced to leave the Badia. Various owners succeed each other over the years.

21st c. The Badia offers overnight accommodations for guests. Courses in Tuscan cooking are held (in English).

Fonterutoli
Marianna's garden

HOW TO ARRIVE

From the Firenze-Siena Superstrada
(motorway), exit San Donato, take
the way to Castellina for about 5
km toward Siena, Loc. Fonterutoli.
Owner: the Mazzei family
Address: Via Puccini 4,
Loc. Fonterutoli, Castellina
in Chianti, Siena
tel.: +39 0577 741385
fax: +39 0577 740676
Visits by appointment only
It is also possible to visit
the wine cellars and sample
the wine

The ancient village in which stands the Villa of Fonterutoli, not far from Castellina in Chianti, was once an Etruscan-Roman settlement, as confirmed by its Latin place name (*Fons Rutilans* or *Fons Rutilii*) and the Etruscan tombs found in the vicinity. Fonterutoli played a major role in the history of the Florence-Siena relationship since it was here, in the early 13th century, that diplomats from the two cities met to try to reach an agreement on the border between their lands.

Particularly interesting are the ancient farm, which has belonged to the Mazzei family since 1435, and the villa, dating from a slightly later time, which has undergone some changes over the course of the centuries (for example, the loggia overlooking the formal garden was added in the early 20th century).

The villa, sober and elegant in appearance, is surrounded by three different gardens: the formal garden, of neo-Medieval style; the rose garden; and the *boschetto* of romantic taste. The three gardens are located in an elongated area that starts in front of the villa.

The **formal garden**, in the shape of an irregular square, is a typical Italian garden with regular sectors bordered by hedges of box.

Probably of late 19th century design, it was restored in the 1930s. From here the visitor, seated under a *berceau* formed of two ancient *Sophora japonica*, can enjoy the splendid panorama of the Sienese Chianti hills.

The villa seen from the garden

The garden is bounded on one side by a high stone wall, shielded by imposing ilexes; the other side opens onto the rose garden.

The rose garden was created at the same time that the formal garden was restored at the wish of the owner of the time, Marianna Mazzei Tommasi Aliotti.

The elongated area is divided into beds of curious shape, planted with clumps of roses and decorated with great citrus urns.

The interesting perspective effect is heightened by a stone arch that forms a backdrop to the entire composition.

High hedges of evergreens (box, viburnum, laurel) separate the modern part of the garden from the little romantic *boschetto*. Narrow, winding paths run through the *boschetto*, shaded by ancient ilexes, as well as plane trees and horse chestnuts planted more recently (*Platanus x acerifolia, Aesculus hippocastanum*) and thickets of bamboo (*Phyllostachis nigra*). In the nearby wine cellars an excellent Chianti classico (*Castello di Fonterutoli*) is still produced, as it was centuries ago.

In one of the little shops in the village perfume and other products coming from the fields of lavender are sold.

To know more

O. Guaita, *Le ville della Toscana*, Rome 1997, pp. 378-380.

I giardini del Chianti, edited by G. Romby, R. Stopani, Florence 1989, p. 109.

Web: www.fonterutoli.com

www.mazzei.it

The formal garden

Giardino Passerini
Farm and garden

HOW TO ARRIVE
Between Cortona and Pergo,
Arezzo or Valdichiana exit from the
Firenze-Roma A1 highway.
Privately owned
Address: La Chiesa 2-4, Pergo, Arezzo
tel.: +39 0575 614052
+39 335 6567252 / +39 335 7062345
e-mail: info@villapasserini.net
The garden is not easy to visit
For information
call the Garden Club of Florence
tel.: +39 055 282245

The Villa of Pergo, lying in the green basin of the Val d'Esse, is surrounded by a beautiful garden dating from the 17th-18th century. The villa is distinguished by its elegant architecture. It was built in the 17th century by the Mancini family (in the chapel is an inscription from 1632 dedicated to Simone Mancini). Later it became the property of the Passerini family, who still own it today.

The layout of the Pergo estate is one of the best examples of that ensemble of rational initiatives carried out by the enlightened landowners of Cortona which, during the course of the 18th century, transformed the Val d'Esse into a great garden.

Pergo appears today, in fact, like an extraordinary agricultural park, structured with great beauty and functionality through broad tree-lined avenues, cultivated fields, walls dividing the orchards, an ornamental gar-

den and beyond it a long *ragnaia*. Through the regular organization of avenues and paths, the countryside enters the garden and blends with it harmoniously.

The entrance to the garden

The gate opens onto a wide avenue where, on the right, stands in all its majestic beauty an ancient **plane tree** (*Platanus orientalis*), declared garden monument and protected by the law on Italy's historical and artistic heritage.

Continuing along the avenue of linden trees in the direction of the villa, we find on the right the large **basin/pool** constructed in 1733. In the shape of a trapezoid, it has a rectangular **artificial island** in the center, linked to the mainland by a double-arched masonry bridge. On the island grow two *Albizzia julibrissin*, silk trees bearing pink flowers.

Beyond the pool, to the right and the left, are two walled gardens, once orchards. Across meadows shaded by tall trees and conifers we go on to arrive at the villa. The building, with its fine interior decorations, is a typical example of villa architecture in the Cortona area.

From the western side of the villa we enter the lovely **formal garden** divided into four beds bordered in box with *Magnolia x soulangeana* trees, a central fountain and a neo-classical *tempietto*. The garden ends at a very unusual building called the *poledraia*, which may once have been used as a stable (it is now a lemon-house). The interior, with cross-vaulted ceiling, is decorated with curious scenes of military life from the Napoleonic era. Behind the villa, in the deepest shade, is a lovely camellia garden sheltered by a *Magnolia grandiflora* and enclosed by walls decorated in *trompe-l'oeil*.

Near the northwest boundary of the estate can still be seen the great *ragnaia* of evergreens used in the 18th century for bird-catching.

The pool with its island

The great plane tree

To know more

M. Pozzana, *I giardini di Cortona*, in "Bollettino Ingegneri", May 1996, n. 5, pp. 3-8.

M. Pozzana, *Toscana, uno sguardo infinito: guida al paesaggio*, Florence 2008.

Web: www.villapasserini.com

the val d'Esse

The ensemble of villas, gardens and cultivated fields that meets the eye of the visitor traversing the Val d'Esse forms a very particular landscape that calls to mind 18th century theories on the *ferme ornée*, or, in a literal translation of the French term, the 'decorative farm'. A *ferme ornée* is an estate made up of farmland, meadows and vineyards, and managed according to principles of utility. Economic and productive requisites are, however, usually brought into harmonious accord with the particular beauty of the places. "Anything that is pretentious, that tends toward the noble, the grand, the majestic, cannot properly appear here". This principle is especially appropriate to the Val d'Esse and its particular features, such as the simple beauty of its villas and the sobriety of the scenery. In 1833 Emanuele Repetti was struck by the landscape with "the perspective of a varied, most pleasant countryside, irrigated by copious perennial springs, sprinkled with country houses and lordly villas amidst numerous rows of vines and olives, not far from forests and boundless fields of grain and artificial prairies".

Il giardino Reinhardt
The garden of Proserpine

HOW TO ARRIVE

Autostrada A1 Firenze-Roma, exit
Valdichiana, direction Sinalunga, take
the Bettolle-Perugia road and exit
onto SP 33, turn onto SS 71
and then follow SP 35 to Pergo.
Address: Loc. Piazzano,
Tuoro sul Trasimeno, Perugia
Tel.: + 39 075 827069
+ 39 3346339496
E-mail: gardinoreinhardt@alice.it
Visting hours: all days from Apr. to the
end of Sept. by appointment only
Admission: 10,00 €
Free admission for under 12,
possibile reduction for groups
Restroom - Restaurant

The labyrinth-garden of exotic plants

In the enchanting Val d'Esse on the border between Umbria and Tuscany, the Reinhardt Garden was created a few years ago. It is one of the few contemporary gardens open to the public in our region. Thomas Reinhardt is a landscape artist, his wife Martina Kofoth a botanist. In 1999 they decided to work on an extraordinary garden composed of three very different parts. The central sector is a **garden of exotic plants** laid out as a labyrinth, where visitors wander through brightly flowering zinnias, hibiscus and marigold, protected by green walls of banana, ficus, and tall reeds, literally engulfed in the wild vegetation of plants. These plants, however, will disappear with the coming of autumn, to be sheltered in greenhouses during the winter. In an incredible metamorphosis, the garden springs alive in good weather, then disappears like Proserpine, only to be born again every spring. On leaving the tropical labyrinth, the visitor traverses a broad grassy avenue framed in a typical mixed border. This is a 'Border of herbaceous and graminaceous perennials', a triumph of plants enclosed at the sides by taller shrubs, according to the classic composition of the English mixed border. Here too, the sense of colour reigns supreme but the landscape of the Val d'Esse, and in the distance the splendid view of stony Cortona stretching over its hillside, form an integral part of the composition designed by the two artists. We go on to the 'Garden under the olive trees', where ancient olive trees are surrounded by herbaceous plants, perennials, alpine flowers and evergreens, mingled with greater attention to form. It is in fact the form of the plants that has led to the creation of this irregular composition, based on paths winding through emerald green meadows of carpeting plants carefully chosen for their globular foliage, harmoniously contrasting with the rolling hills of the terrain. In July, thanks to the Reinhardt Park and Garden Society, the garden is open to all lovers of plants and botany for two days; rare and exotic plants are on sale.

To know more

Web: www.giardinoreinhardt.com

Villa Sandrelli
The peasant and his wife in the garden

HOW TO ARRIVE

The Valdichiana exit from the Firenze-Roma A1 highway.
Owners: Alberto Sandrelli and Maria Sofia Sandrelli Duranti
Address: Via Lauretana 1, Camucia, Arezzo
tel.: +39 0575 603128
Visiting hours: by appointment only
Accessible to the disabled

The formal garden

Built in the first half of the 18th century by a descendent of Marsilio Tommasi, the villa is situated in the center of Camucia; at the time it was built it was almost the only house in the village.

The pretty garden, covering about half a hectare, was created from 1753 to 1764 (the work was amply documented in a notebook of accounts kept by the owners), while the villa was completed in 1749 and the two side wings in 1777. Beside the main body of the villa are a little *limonaia* and the farm.

The garden, although changed over the course of time, still clearly shows today its original 18th century structure.

Enclosed by a wall decorated with terra-cotta vases and sculptures, the part nearest the villa was transformed in the late 19th century by the addition of informal flower beds and tall trees.

In 1928, at the time when the estate passed into the hands of the Sandrelli family, the 18th century *pomario* was also transformed, becoming an **ornamental garden** with hedges and clipped spheres of box (the tuje were planted at an even more recent time).

Lying on a gentle slope, the small garden of the villa is laid out in two parts, the one nearest to the house composed of the flower garden and *pomario*; the other, lower down and linked by a stairway, occupied by a *ragnaia* and the orchard. Originally the two areas clearly coincided with the different uses of the garden itself: one more closely linked to villa life and to 'enjoyment', the other to agriculture and utility.

On the wall enclosing the lower part of the garden are two wall-fountains with calcareous decorations now unfortunately ruined. In the two niches stand the figures of the *Villanella*, or peasant woman, holding a basket of fruit, and the *Villano*, or peasant, in popular costumes, both typical personages of 18th century garden decoration. The niche with the *Villano* has been changed by the addition of a clock.

Parco Tommasi Aliotti
A miniature villa Marlia

HOW TO ARRIVE

In the vicinity of Camucia,
Valdichiana exit from the Firenze-
Roma A1 highway.
Owner: the Tommasi Aliotti family
Address: Case Sparse 639,
Loc. Metelliano, Cortona, Arezzo
tel.: +39 0575 603394
Guided visits upon request
in Summer, at the owner's discretion
Accessible to the disabled
Restrooms not for disabled

The corridor of ilexes behind the villa

Ferdinando Chiostri, in his book on Tuscan parks, compares this villa to that of Marlia for the breadth and scope of its natural scenery. He is struck by the fascination of the place, the *genius loci* that confers on the estate a beauty and majesty enhanced still further by the lovely pond lying before it. "Beautiful is the basin in front of the villa", notes Chiostri, "an embellishment certainly not very ancient, but one which notably contributes to the beauty of this place".

The villa, an elegant three-storey building with a very simple facade bounded to the east by a fine chapel and to the west by a *limonaia* of exotic style, owes its fascination both to its position and to the transformations carried out during the course of the 19th century, on the basis of the existing 18th century structure. Niccolò Tommasi created the present villa by radically renovating, in the second half of the 18th century, a property that already existed in the 16th century. The accounts listing his expenses include, in 1774, costs for "having rebuilt half of the house to be used as villa, a chapel, and half of the peasant's house, about one thousand six hundred *scudi* at least".

In the following century Luigi Tommasi (1827-1903) transformed the estate into an English garden, planting a fine collection of trsees and adding numerous decorative features. Still today, amid examples of *Sequoiadendron giganteum*, *Abies pinsapo* and *Cupressus funebris*, we find stone benches, rock gardens and a *romitorio*.

To the sides of the entrance avenue, now lined with cypresses, vast farmlands stretch out within the park. The avenue leads to the pond, then divides to run along two great flower beds where pink peonies explode in blossom.

Behind the villa is an imposing **cerchiata** of ancient ilexes. A lovely path meanders through the great park around it.

Villa Guillichini
Warriors in the garden

HOW TO ARRIVE

Not far from Arezzo, Montevarchi exit from the Firenze-Roma A1 highway.
Privately owned: the villa has been divided into apartments, separately owned
Address: Tregozzano, Arezzo
Visiting hours: the garden, recently restored, cannot be visited easily
Information: Department of Architectural Assets and Landscape, for the Historic, Artistic and Ethno-anthropological Heritage of the Province of Arezzo,
Via Ricasoli 1, Arezzo, tel.: +39 0575 40901, +39 0575 409044

The geometric parterre

Villa Guillichini, located at Tregozzano near Arezzo, is surrounded by one of the most important gardens in the area.

Near the end of the 16th century the building belonged to Francesco di Agnolo Guillichini. It was described as an "estate of lands cultivated to vineyards, orchards and a portion to olive and mulberry trees, with the manor house". In the first half of the 17th century the villa belonged to Lodovico di Francesco Guillichini, juryconsult and professor of civil institutions at Pisa as well as Knight of Santo Stefano. Lodovico had the chapel of Santo Stefano built, adjacent to the villa but for public use, already around the middle of the century. In 1730 Rosa Guillichini Berardi sold the estate to her sons. At the death of the two ecclesiastics, the property was inherited by their nephew Angiolo (1736-1814). It was Angiolo who first enlarged the villa by encapsulating at the back the most ancient part and extending the left side of the building by adding to it a short wing. In the 19th century the villa, owned first by Giovan Francesco and then by his son Luigi, underwent further renovation, particularly on the occasion of the wedding of Luigi and Marianna Albergotti.

Dating from 1831 is the layout of the park with its **parterre** and the formal garden below, once adorned with statues. The construction of the right wing used as *limonaia*, of the theater and the planting of the surrounding woods date instead from 1873. In 1880, on the occasion of the sale by Giovan Battista to his brothers, the villa, the *boschetto,* the *ragnaia* and the citrus trees were assessed. Also listed was "the portion of lawn that lies before the two buildings... a portion of land kept as vineyard where there exist several low Grapevines and various Fruit Trees, some benches, three terra-cotta Statues, a Column with an eagle, and various pilasters encrusted with glass and marble, plus a Room for keeping Flower vases". Many of these elements no longer exist today.

Created in the course of the 19th century, the garden and park ensemble stretches over a sloping hillside. The formal garden contains beds bordered in box with a pool at the center; located in front of the house, it is enclosed by a wall and preceded by unusual towers serving as guard post (it is easy to imagine two armed warriors rushing out of the towers to defend the garden). Majestic trees stand in the English garden, distinguished by an outdoor theatrical space with a fine 19th century construction serving as backdrop.

Other gardens in Tuscany

Castello di Belcaro
Loc. Belcaro, Siena - tel.: +39 0577 394237 - The garden is now undergoing restoration and visits will not be possible in brief periods.

A lovely forest of ancient ilexes surrounds the castle rebuilt in 1525, perhaps by Baldassarre Peruzzi. Within the wall lies the lemon garden with urns scattered over the lawn.

Castello di Cafaggiolo
Via Nazionale 16 - Barberino di Mugello, Florence - tel.: +39 055 8498103
Visiting hours: from April 15 to October 15 Wed. and Fri. - Sun. 2:30 pm - 6:30 pm, Sat. - Sun. also 10:00 am - 12.30 pm; from Oct. 16 to Apr. 14: Sat. - Sun. 10:00 am - 12:30 pm, 2:30 pm - 6:30 pm
www.castellodicafaggiolo.it - info@castellodicafaggiolo.it

The Medicean castle, rebuilt in the early 15th century by Michelozzo di Bartolomeo, conserves only the plan of the Renaissance garden, totally transformed in the 19th century. Today it contains tall trees, ancient mulberries and a sequoia.

Castello di Montegufoni
Via di Montegufoni 20, Montagnana val di Pesa, Florence
tel.: +39 0571 671131 - Privately owned - Visits are not allowed
www.montegufoni.it

The garden, not large in size, consists of hedges of cypress and box planted by the English Sitwell family, owners of the magnificent castle for three generations. The 18th c. grotto inspired by the myth of Galatea with automata once moved by hydraulic mechanisms is highly interesting. The castle is used for country tourism.

Certosa di Pontignano
S.S. 408 in the direction of Pianella, Loc. Pontignano, Vagliagli, Siena
tel.: +39 0577 35471 - visits are possible for groups and schools only and by reservation via fax - www.pontignano.unisi.it - certosa@unisi.it

The monastery, founded in 1343, was sold in 1784 to the hermits of Monte Celso and then to the Sergardi family. Today it is owned by the University of Siena, which organizes conferences and seminars there. The garden retains some of its original features, such as the rectangular fishpond and the *ragnaia* of clipped ilexes for bird-catching on the northern side. Fine collection of potted lemon trees.

Le Corti
Via San Piero di Sotto 1, San Casciano, Florence - tel.: +39 055 829301
visiting hours: from April to October (except August) Tuesday - Thursday by appointment - www.principecorsini.com - info@principecorsini.com

A monumental avenue of cypresses leads to the beautiful villa. The garden consists of a broad lawn around the house, a *boschetto* behind it and a terrace with flower beds.

Orto botanico di Lucca
Via del Giardino botanico 14, Lucca
tel.: +39 0583 583086 - fax: +39 0583 56738
visiting hours: from January 1 to March 18 and from November 3 to December 31 by appointment Mon. - Fri. 9:30 am - 12:30 pm; from March 19 to April 30 and from September 15 to November 2 10:00 am - 5:00 pm; from May 1 to June 30 10:00 am - 6:00 pm; from July 1 to September 14 10:00 am - 7:00 pm - Admission: 3,00 € ; 2,00 € reduced - E-mail: ortobotanico@lunet.it

Founded in 1820 by Maria Luisa di Borbone, the garden has an arboretum, a hillock and a pond, as well as a botanical school and greenhouses. Important collections of medicinal plants, rhododendrons, camellias and spontaneous botanical species used in the Lucchese cuisine.

Orto botanico di Pisa
Via Luca Ghini 5, Pisa - tel.: +39 050 2211313 - fax: +39 050 2211309
visiting hours: Mon. - Fri. 8:30 am - 5:00 pm, Sat. 8:30 am - 1:00 pm
Admission: 2,50 €; 1,50 € reduced
www.biologia.unipi.it/ortobotanico - ortomuseobot@biologia.unipi.it

Luca Ghini founded the Orto in 1544, when Cosimo I summoned him to take the chair of botany at the University of Pisa. This is Europe's oldest botanical garden. In 1591 the Orto was moved to its present location, between Via Santa Maria and Via Roma, by Giuseppe Casabona. In 1752 the facade of the gallery was transformed by the addition of decorations in *pietra spugna* and calcareous concretions typical of 16th century grottoes. In the Orto grow centuries-old trees: a *Magnolia grandiflora* and a *Ginkgo biloba* planted in 1787, a *Platanus occidentalis* from 1808, a myrtle planted in 1815 and a camphor tree (*Cinnamomum camphora*) introduced around 1842. Of extraordinary historical and scientific importance are the naturalist collections and the herbarium of dried plants (*Herbarium Horti Pisani*).

Above:
the theater
of Villa
Bernardini

Bottom:
the garden
of the Certosa
di Pontignano

Poggio Torselli

Via Scopeti 10, San Casciano in val di Pesa, Florence
tel.: +39 338 3592353, +39 055 8290241, +39 055 8229557
visiting hours: by appointment for groups minimum 25 persons
Admission: 25,00 € for villa, park and garden
Wine sampling, buffets and dinners can also be booked
www.poggiotorselli.it - poggiotorselli@telematicaitalia.it

Poggio Torselli at San Casciano has now opened its garden, recently restored with great care, even salvaging the ancient irrigation system. The blossoming of the flowers in spring is magnificent.

Roseto botanico Carla Fineschi

Loc. Casalone 76, Cavriglia, Arezzo - tel.: +39 366 2063941
visiting hours: from the first Sun. of May to the last Sun. of June
9:00 am - 7:00 pm by appointment - Admission: € 5,00
www.rosetofineschi.it - info@rosetofineschi.it

The most important collection of roses in Italy, created by the owner Gianfranco Fineschi in decades of ardent collecting, containing thousands of species and varieties.

Torre Guinigi

Via Sant'Andrea (palazzo Guinigi), Lucca
tel.: +39 0583 583086 - fax: +39 0583 56738 - visiting hours: all days
Jan. - Feb. and Nov. - Dec. 9:30 am - 4:30 pm; Mar. and Oct. 9:30 am - 5:30 pm; Apr. - May 9:30 am - 6:30 pm; Jun. - Sep. 9:30 am - 7:30 pm
Admission: 3,50 €; 2,50 € reduced

A garden or rather a *boschetto* of ilexes planted on the terrace of a tower that dominates the whole city. The garden was used by members of the family as a delightful place of repose.

Villa Bernardini

Via di Vicopelago 573/A, Vicopelago, Lucca
tel.: +39 328 8238199 - tel. e fax: +39 0583 370327
visiting hours: only in Summer Mon. - Fri. 9:00 am - 12:30 am,
3:00 pm - 7:00 pm - www.villabernardini.it - info@villabernardini.it

A fine late Renaissance villa completed in 1615 by the Bernardini family (as indicated by the inscription over the front doorway). The villa is surrounded by a large park with *limonaia* and a fine garden theater in box clipped in spherical shapes, dating from the mid-18th-century.

Villa Borrini

Pieve di Compito, Lucca
tel.: +39 0583 428418 (Municipality of Capannori, Tourism Bureau)
open to visitors only during the exhibition *Ancient Camellias of Lucchesia*, held in March
www.camelielucchesia.it - info@camelielucchesia.it

This lovely 19th century villa, usually not open to the public, is surrounded by a stupendous garden of camellias. In the immediate vicinity of the villa, at Sant'Andrea di Compito, is the nursery of Guido Cattolica, a descendent of the Borrini family. Ancient camellia trees grow here, as well as the original species and varieties of the villa garden.

Villa Gori Muratori Ginanneschi

Strada di Ventena 8/10, Siena - tel.: +39 0577 44705
Visiting hours: by appointment only

Important 'garden theater' with stage paved in pebble mosaic. The theater is linked to the villa by an ancient avenue of ilexes. A second ilex avenue leads to the 'garden maze'.

Villa di Gricigliano

Via di Gricigliano 52, loc. Gricigliano, Pontassieve, Florence
tel.: +39 055 8309622 - www.icrsp.org - info@icrsp.org

Usually not open to the public, the imposing villa, dating from the 16th century, is surrounded by a broad moat filled with water. The great exedra-shaped lawn was once a *cavallerizza*, an area used for horse racing. Other interesting features are a terraced garden with wall-fountain, an elegant nymphaeum and a *loggia*; to the north is a great *selvatico* of ilex trees. The villa, once the property of the Martelli family, is now owned by the religious order of the Sacro Cuore di Gesù Redentore. In the nearby 18th century chapel, it is possible to participate in the sung mass and Gregorian chant.

Villa I Busini

Castiglioni di Rufina, Loc. Scopeti 28, Florence - tel.: +39 055 8397809
Visiting hours: by appointment only

The villa originated in the 15th century; enlarged over the years, in the early 20th century it was embellished by a fine formal garden built over an existing system of terraces. The villa is now used for country tourism.

Villa La Pescigola

Loc. Pescigola, Fivizzano, Massa - tel.: +39 0585 927109, +39 0187 610312, +39 340 8556213 - visiting hours: from March 27 to May 1 Sat. - Sun. 10:00 am - 7:00 pm. - other days visit by appontment only - Admission: 5,00 €; reduced for children and families - www.villapescigola.com

In the vicinity of Fivizzano, the 18th-c. residence of the Adami family has been opening its garden every year for six years for the Narcissus Festival. The great 18th c. parterre was recreated with thousands of narcissus in bloom for the festival held from March 27 to May 1.

Villa di Meleto

Via Meleto 19, Castelnuovo d'Elsa, Castelfiorentino, Florence
tel. e fax: +39 0571 673137 - Visiting hours: holiday house, by appointment only - www.villameleto.com - villameleto@libero.it

An Italian garden with fine box beds created at the turn of the century over 18th century terraces. In the 19th century Cosimo Ridolfi introduced new systems of experimental agriculture.

Villa Puccini

Via Dalmazia, Pistoia - tel.: +39 0573 371688, +39 055 0573 371698 (Cultural and Tourism Bureau, Municipality of Pistoia) - Free admission visiting hours: always open (for the villa by appointment only via e-mail to cultura@comune.pistoia.it)

The great park was created by Luigi de Cambray Digny and in part belongs to the City of Pistoia, which has opened it to the public. The romantic pond with tempietto is especially interesting.

Villa Roncioni

Strada Sotto Monte in the vicinity of San Giuliano Terme, Pisa.
tel.: +39 050 819283, +39 050 819248 (Municipality of San Giuliano Terme, Cultural Bureau) - the garden is now undergoing restoration

An interesting park created in the first half of the 19th-century by Alessandro della Gherardesca, who designed the neo-Gothic building where silk worms were raised.

Villa Rucellai

Via di Canneto 16, Prato - tel.: +39 0574 460392 - fax: +39 0574 467748
Visiting hours: by appointment for groups maximum 10 persons
www.villarucellai.com - canneto@masternet.it

This beautiful villa, now used as a hotel, grew up around a Medieval tower. It has a fine terraced formal garden with boxwood topiaries, offering a magnificent view over the valley of the Bisenzio.

Villa Varramista

Via Ricavo, Loc. Varramista, Montopoli in Valdarno, Pisa - tel.: +39 0571 44711
fax: +39 0571 447216 - visiting hours: from May 1 to Oct. 31 9:00 am - 6:00 pm; from Nov. 1 to Apr. 30 10.00 am - 4:00 pm - Admission: 7,00 €; 5,00 € reduced - www.varramista.it - info@varramista.it

Owned by the Capponi family since 1953, is a large building planned by Buontalenti, surrounded by formal gardens (remodelled by Pietro Porcinai) and a great park.

Flower shows and exhibitions

Borgo a Mozzano (Lucca)
Azalea show *(April).*

Chianciano Terme (Siena)
Villa La Foce
Events in the Territory of Siena *(July and August)*
(event included in the Grandi Giardini Italiani circuit).

Firenze
Giardino dell'Iris
Iris show (*April-May*).

Giardino dell'Orticoltura
Flower show (*April 25 - May 1, Autumn*).
Tuscan nurseries participate.

Palazzo Budini Gattai
Camellia show (*end of March*).

Fivizzano (Massa)
Villa La Pescigola
Festival of the Narcissus (*from late March to early May*) - (included in the Grandi Giardini Italiani circuit).

Lastra a Signa (Florence)
Parco Vivai Belfiore
Pomarium: market fair of ancient and rare fruit trees (*early September*).

Lucca
Villa Oliva
Exhibition of topiary art (*June*).

Along the walls of the city
Murabilia (*september*). Nurseries from all over Italy participate.

Pescia (Pistoia)
Biennale flower show (*September*).
Dedicated to cut flowers.

Pieve di Compito (Lucca)
Camellia show (biennale, *March*).

Glossary

Aviary A great cage often in the form of a pavilion where exotic birds are kept.

Balustrade Balustrades usually consist of small shaped columns forming parapets.

Baroque garden A 17th-18th century garden which interprets in a particularly theatrical manner the perspectives of the 16th century garden.

Bowling-green A lawn of rectangular shape used in English gardens for bowling (or other outdoor games).

Boschetto A small grove of trees.

Cabreo list of holdings or property illustrated by detailed maps.

English garden An informal landscape garden which became popular all over Europe in the 19th century.

Fabrique French term for the little constructions widely used in 18th century parks: *tempietti*, grottoes, pavilions and so on.

Fagianeria A fenced-in area with annexed construction where pheasants were raised.

Flower garden An enclosed, protected area in which flowers are grown. For Renaissance gardens the term *secret garden* is also used (see).

Formal garden (see *Italian garden*).

French garden A garden created according to the rules of perspective and decoration developed in France in the 17th century. It is distinguished by avenues bordered by elaborate *parterres de broderie* (see) and *boschetti* clipped in shapes.

Gabinetto di roccaglia Italian for *cabinet de rocaille*, a restricted space adorned by rock gardens.

Gamberaia A pool for crayfish raised for the kitchen. A place name recurrently found in Tuscany derives from the name of the pool.

Garden of acclimatization Garden of scientific nature in which exotic plants are grown to study their adaptability to a different climate.

Garden room (see *stanza di verzura*)

Garenna (or rabbit island) An artificial island in the center of a pool or pond where rabbits were kept during the Baroque period.

Giardino dei Semplici Garden of medicinal herbs. From the Medieval Latin *medicamentum simplex*: "medicine made with herbs".

Grotto Garden architecture designed to imitate natural caves. Very frequently used starting from the early 16th century. It often has a vaulted ceiling decorated with pietre spugne and other materials (see *polimaterico*).

Italian garden (or *formal garden*) A geometric garden of limited size. Widespread in Europe in the early 20th century, in coincidence with the revival of the Renaissance Italian garden.

Jardin potager The French term for orchard or vegetable garden.

Lawn Broad grassy area often located in front of the villa; heightens the effect of the building.

Limonaia (or *stanzone* for citrus trees) A rectangular building where citrus trees are sheltered in cold weather. A lemon garden is often found in front of it.

Mascaron Human or animal head, often deformed in grotesque style, used from Renaissance times on for the decoration of fountains.

Nymphaeum Grotto inspired by Roman nymphaeums, places sacred to water nymphs.

Parterre Group of flower beds. The etymology of the term is uncertain; it either derives from the Latin *partiri*, to divide into sections, or from the French *par terre*, "on the ground". *Parterre de broderie* is the French term used to indicate beds of particularly elegant design, recalling lacework; used in the classic French garden from the 17th-century on.

Polimaterico Type of decoration used in Renaissance and Baroque grottoes, formed of various materials: marble, pietre spugne, shells, ceramic elements and so on.

Ragnaia A little wood of clipped evergreens where nets were stretched to catch birds.

Romitorio A building often in the form of a ruin designed to call to mind a hermit's dwelling place.

Rustic decoration Decoration made of rough-hewn stones or pietre spugne taken from natural caves.

Secret garden An enclosed, protected area where flowers are grown. For Renaissance gardens the term *flower garden* is also used (see).

Selvatico (or *salvatico*, archaic) A *boschetto* (see) of evergreen trees, often ilexes, contrasting with the ornamental garden with its flowers, beds and hedges.

Spugna (or *pietra spugna*) Calcareous concretions coming from natural caves; used to decorate grottoes.

Stanza di verzura (or Garden room) A part of the garden bounded by hedges or rows of trees. From this term derives the expression 'giardino a stanze' or 'a camere', that is composed of various garden rooms.

Teatro di verzura (or Garden theater) A garden room (see) designed like a theater.

Topiary The art of clipping trees and shrubs in geometric ornamental shapes

Verzura Archaic term indicating vegetation.

Analytical index

Abakanowicz, Magdalena, 110
Acciaiuoli, Alessandro, 30
Acton, Arthur, 58
Acton, Harold, 58
Aeppli, Eva, 146
Alberti, Leon Battista, 5
Aldobrandini, family, 158
Aldobrandini, Luisa, 158
Alfieri, Vittorio, 161
Amati, family, 115
Ambroziewicz, Mariano, 58
Ammannati, Bartolomeo, 10, 12, 34, 52, 53, 54, 55, 87
Antinori Aldobrandini, Maria, 157
Anzilotti, Rolando, 104
Attavanti, Pandolfo, 114
Aulenti, Gae, 118
Austin, David, 142
Baccani, Gaetano, 28, 29, 30
Baciocchi, Elisa, 126, 127
Bandinelli, Baccio, 16
Bardini, Stefano, 19, 20, 22, 23
    Ugo, 19, 20, 23
Barni, Roberto, 146
Berenson, Bernard, 47, 70, 77, 169
Bernardini, family, 185
Bianchi Bandinelli, family, 161
    Domenico, 160
Bimbi, Bartolomeo, 56
Blundell Spence, William, 77
Bonaiuti, Pasquale, 58
Bonazza, Antonio, 58
Bonazza, Giovanni, 58
Bonazza, Tommaso, 58
Borbone, Maria Luisa, 184
Botta, Mario, 144
Bourget, Paul, 93
Budini Gattai, family, 34
Buonarroti, Michelangelo, 15, 16, 94
Buontalenti, Bernardo, 10, 12, 16, 18, 30, 84, 85, 87, 189
Buonvisi, family, 122, 127, 130, 136
Buren, David, 115
Cacialli, Giuseppe, 13, 17
Campion, Jane, 140
Cappello, Bianca, 32, 33
Capponi, family, 47, 58, 60, 65

Ferdinando Carlo, 44
    Gino, 44, 47
Caruso, Enrico, 88, 89
Casanova, Giacomo, 154
Castellucci, Giuseppe, 39, 58, 92
Catastini, family, 120
Cattani, family, 102
Celsi, family, 156
    Mino, 156
Cerati, Antonio (Filandro Cretense), 130, 134
Chigi, family, 150, 153, 154, 155
    Flavio, 150
Ciaccheri, Giuliano, 88
Cioli, Valerio, 16
Civitali, Matteo, 135
Clifford, Henry, 45, 47
Clusio, Carlo, 40
Cohen, Gil, 142
Consagra, Pietro, 105
Controni, family, 140
Coronati, Giulio, 102
Corsi, family, 24, 78, 81
Corsini, family, 30, 31, 50, 95
Craige, Sheppard, 170, 171
Cutting, Sybil, lady Scott of Ancrum, 44, 47, 49, 77
Dapples, Luigi, 102, 103
da Sangallo, Giuliano, 38, 90
da Vinci, Pierino, 52, 57
De Cambray Digny, Luigi, 26, 29, 33, 87, 186
de Saint Phalle, Niki, 7, 144, 145
del Riccio, Agostino, 29
Del Rosso, Giuseppe, 15
Del Rosso, Zanobi, 11, 13, 15, 17, 18
del Tadda, Giovanni Battista, 16
della Gherardesca, Alessandro, 186
della Gherardesca, Ersilia, 23
Demidoff, Maria, 85, 87
di Andrea Lapi, Zanobi, 60, 65
di Bartolomeo, Michelozzo, 76, 77, 100, 184
di Bicci, Giovanni, 100
di Collobiano, Oliva, 30
di Zanobi di Pagno, Raffaello, 51
Dodge, Edwin, 58

Dosio, Giovanni Antonio, 89
Eleonora di Toledo, 10, 15, 18
Fallani, Bernardo, 29
Fancelli, Giovanni, 16
Favreau, Pietro, 65
Fedi, Pio, 28
Ferretti, Giovan Domenico, 114
Ferrucci, Romolo, 17
Ficino, Marsilio, 92
Foggini, Giovan Battista, 87, 95
Fontana, Carlo, 150
Fortini, Davide, 10, 16, 18, 57, 90
Frescobaldi, family, 117
    Anastasia, 117
Frietsch, Joseph, 51, 57, 82, 87
Gaeta, Giuseppe, 173
Galeotti, Paolo, 57
Gamberai, Antonio, 115
Gamberelli, family, 63, 65
Gambini, Giovanni, 110, 113
Garzoni, family, 107
    Romano, 106
Garzoni, Giovanna, 40
Gervais, Paul, 142
Ghini, Luca, 36, 184
Giambologna, 13, 17, 18, 33, 48, 51, 52, 54, 55, 83, 84, 85
Ginori, family, 98
Giovannozzi, Pietro, 66
Giovannozzi, Ugo, 72
Gori, Giuliano, 110, 113
Grabau, family, 137
Gréber, Jacques, 122, 127
Greco, Emilio, 104
Grifoni, Ugolino, 34
Guasti, Marcello, 7, 149
Guicciardini Corsi Salviati, family, 78
    Giulio, 81
Guillichini, family, 183
Guinigi, Bernardino, 122
Hamilton Finlay, Jan, 112
Inoue, Bukichi, 112, 113
Juvarra, Filippo, 107, 128
Keshko, Catherine Jeanne, Princess Ghyka, 60, 64, 65
Kofoth, Martina, 180

Lambton, Lord Anthony, 153

Lansing, Frances, 171

Lasinio, Ferdinando, 51

Le Blanc, Jacques-Louis, 20, 22, 23

Le Nôtre, André, 130

Leoni, Diomede, 164, 165

Linaker, Arturo, 94

Lorena, family, 10, 87
  Ferdinando III, 57, 82, 87
  Leopoldo II, 55, 57, 173
  Pietro Leopoldo, 15

Lorenzi, Stoldo, 13, 15

Lusini, Enrico, 94

Malatesta, Anna Elena, 24

Manadori, family, 23

Mancini, family, 178

Manetti, Giuseppe, 24, 25, 94

Marinali, Orazio, 58

Martini, Georg Cristoph, 128

Mazzei, family, 176

Mazzei Tommasi Aliotti,
  Marianna, 177

Mazzuoli, Giuseppe, 150, 152,
  153, 164

Medici, family, 50, 66, 100, 114
  Cosimo il Vecchio, 24, 100
  Cosimo I, 10, 18, 24, 37, 34, 36, 37,
    47, 52, 57, 77, 90, 114, 184
  Cosimo II, 12, 37, 38, 47
  Cosimo III, 55, 77, 164
  Ferdinando I, 51, 57, 87
  Francesco I, 32, 82, 87, 114
  Giovan Carlo, 32, 33, 40
  Giovanni, later Pope Leo X, 175
  Giovanni di Cosimo, 76
  Lorenzo il Magnifico, 38, 77, 90,
    91, 94, 100

Melotti, Fausto, 111

Messeri, Luigi, 65

Micheli, Pier Antonio, 27, 37, 47

Micheli Pietro, 27

Milani, Luigi Adriano, 38, 39

Mitoraj, Igor, 13

Molder, Ignazio, 161

Morel, Jean Marie, 126

Moriconi, family, 140

Morris, Richard, 111

Mozzi, family, 19, 20, 22, 23

Muti, Riccardo, 72

Naccherino, Michelangelo, 17

Nagasawa, Hidetoshi, 112, 115

Novelli, Antonio, 33

Oppenheim, Denis, 111

Orford, Margherita, lady, 23, 77

Origo, Iris, 167, 168, 169

Orsetti, family, 127

Panciatichi, family, 114

Paoletti, Niccolò Gaspero, 11, 13, 17,
  18, 77

Paolo da Montemigliaio, 175

Parigi, Alfonso, il Giovane, 10, 32

Parigi, Giulio, 10, 15, 18

Parlatore, Filippo, 17

Partini, Giuseppe, 172

Passeri, Gerolamo, 95

Passerini, family, 178

Pepper, Beverly, 112

Pericoli, Niccolò, known as Tribolo,
  10, 18, 36, 51, 52, 53, 54, 57, 90

Peruzzi, Baldassarre, 6, 154, 155,
  156, 162, 184

Peyron, Angelo, 72

Peyron, Paolo, 72, 74

Pfanner, Felice, 140

Piccolomini, Enea Silvio, later Pope
  Pius II, 166

Piccolomini Silvio, 166

Pinsent, Cecil Ross, 6, 45, 47, 68, 70,
  77, 167, 168, 169

Poccianti, Pasquale, 11, 13, 17, 90

Poggi, Giuseppe, 33, 95

Poirier, Anne e Patrick, 115

Porcinai, Martino, 65

Porcinai, Pietro, 7, 65, 94, 104, 112,
  120, 121, 162, 186

Pozzana, Mariachiara, 148

Pozzolini, family, 98

Pucci, Alessandro, 89

Pucci, Antonio, 29

Pucci, family, 118

Pucci, Orazio Ruberto, 88

Rapi, Sebastiano, 66

Reinhardt, Thomas, 180

Repetti, Emanuele, 114, 179

Ricasoli, family, 172, 173, 175
  Bettino, 172, 173
  Vincenzo, 172, 173

Ridolfi, Cosimo, 116, 117, 186

Rinieri, family, 95

Romoli, Francesco, 38

Rossellino, Bernardo, 166

Roster, Giacomo, 94

Rucellai, Bernardo, 32, 33

Salvini, Sebastiano, 15

Sandrelli, family, 181

Santini, Nicolao, 130

Santini, Vittoria, 130

Savi, Pietro, 116

Scaretti, Lorenzo, 100

Scaretti Jebb, Marjorie, 100, 101

Scott, Geoffrey, 68, 70, 77

Scott, lady, see Cutting, Sybil

Serristori, ser Jacopo, 92

Silvani, Gherardo, 23, 30, 81

Silvani, Pier Francesco, 33, 66

Sitwell, family, 184

Socini, Agenore, 102, 103

Spoerri, Daniel, 7, 146, 147

Staccioli, Mauro, 112

Stibbert, Frederick, 95

Stiozzi Ridolfi, Giuseppe, 33

Strong, Charles Augustus, 68

Susini, Francesco, 12, 18

Tacca, Pietro, 15

Targioni Tozzetti, Antonio, 29

Targioni Tozzetti, Ottaviano, 37

Taylor, Myron, 95

Tinguely, Jean, 145

Tintori, family, 57

Tommasi, family, 181, 182

Topor, Roland, 146

Torrigiani, family, 28
  Pietro, 26, 28, 29
  Pietro Guadagni, 130

Ubertini, Francesco, known as
  Bachiacca, 54

Utens, Justus, 6, 18, 48, 55, 57, 90,
  101, 114

Varchi, Benedetto, 52

Vasari, Giorgio, 10, 16, 52

Venturi, Venturino, 105

Watson, H. O., 58

Wharton, Edith, 159

Zocchi, Giuseppe, 115

Index of gardens

Badia a Coltibuono, 174
Boboli, 10
Castello di Barberino
   di Mugello, 102
Castello di Belcaro, 184
Castello di Brolio, 172
Castello di Cafaggiolo, 184
Castello di Celsa, 156
Castello di Montegufoni, 184
Castello del Trebbio, 100
Certosa di Pontignano, 184
Fonte Lucente, 72
Fonterutoli, 176
Geggiano, 160
Giardino Bardini, 19
Giardino Budini Gattai, 34
Giardino Capponi, 44
Giardino di Castello, 52
Giardino Corsi (or Annalena), 24
Giardino Corsini al Prato, 30
Giardino Garzoni, 106
Giardino di Granaiolo, 118
Giardino dell'Iris, 94
Giardino del Museo
   archeologico, 38
Giardino dell'Orticoltura, 94
Giardino di Palazzo
   Piccolomini, 6, 166
Giardino Passerini, 6, 178
Garden of Daniel Spoerri, 7, 146
Giardino Reinhardt, 7, 180
Giardino dei Tarocchi, 7, 144
Giardino Torrigiani, 6, 26
Horti Leonini, 164
I Collazzi, 94
L'Apparita, 7, 162
La Foce, 7, 167
La Ragnaia
   di San Giovanni d'Asso, 7, 170
Le Balze, 7, 68
Le Corti, 184
Orti Oricellari, 32, 40
Orto botanico di Firenze, 36
Orto botanico di Lucca, 184
Orto botanico di Pisa, 184
Palazzo Medici Riccardi, 94

Palazzo Pfanner, 140
Palazzo Strozzi al Boschetto, 94
Palazzo Vivarelli Colonna, 94
Parco delle Cascine, 94
Parco di Celle, 110
Parco del Neto, 94
Parco di Pinocchio, 104
Parco della Sterpaia, 148
Parco Tommasi Aliotti, 182
Poggio a Caiano, 90
Poggio Torselli, 185
Parco di Pratolino, 6, 82
Roseto botanico Carla Fineschi, 185
Torre Guinigi, 185
Villa di Bellosguardo, 88
Villa Bernardini, 185
Villa Bibbiani, 116
Villa di Bivigliano, 98
Villa Borrini, 185
Villa Buonvisi Oliva, 134
Villa Casagrande, 92
Villa di Careggi, 94
Villa il Castelluccio, 7, 120
Villa Cetinale, 150
Villa Corsi Salviati, 78
Villa Corsini a Castello, 95
Villa Gamberaia, 6, 56, 60
Villa Gori Muratori
   Ginanneschi, 185
Villa Grabau, 125, 137
Villa di Gricigliano, 186
Villa Guillichini, 183
Villa I Busini, 186
Villa I Tatti, 7, 70
Villa La Magia, 7, 114
Villa La Pescigola, 186
Villa La Pietra, 58
Villa La Quiete, 66
Villa Mansi, 41, 128
Villa di Marlia, 6, 122
Villa Massei, 142
Villa Medici, 76, 169
Villa di Meleto, 186
Villa della Petraia, 48
Villa Puccini, 186
Villa Roncioni, 186
Villa il Roseto, 7

Villa Rucellai, 186
Villa Sandrelli, 181
Villa Schifanoia, 95
Villa Stibbert, 95
Villa Torrigiani, 130
Villa Varramista, 186
Villa il Ventaglio, 95
Villa di Vicobello, 154